The Thoughts I Still See

By Michelle J.E. Temple

Copyright of Michelle J.E. Temple

Dedication

To all those who get up every morning and keep trying. Whether it be physical pain or emotional pain, I see you and I feel you. We are not alone.

Preface

This book starts at a halfway point through one of the darkest periods of my life. I have just completed 17 Transcranial magnetic stimulation treatment days. I wanted this book to be about recovery from Harm OCD and Depression, but the truth is I don't know when my recovery actually ends. At the same time, I am struggling with menopause and other physical issues. This is about trying to do better every day, falling back, and getting up and trying again. This is a true story I'm certain that others with mental illness or those overwhelmed with life will see in themselves. This is a raw purge of my thoughts and struggles as I try to come to terms with recovering and living with mental illness.

TMS Session 18

It's a Monday morning in mid-February, a dark cold morning in our little part of the prairie. I wake up at 6:30 a.m. and stumble over to the coffee pot. I have never in my life been an early riser, but for some reason my thoughts have started waking me up at 4:30 or 5:30, then I go ahead and get out of bed at 6:30. I have some coffee and sit on the couch and look out at the frozen icicles on the trees. It's dark but our Christmas lights are still on and the icicles glow with tinges of red and green. I have the biggest weight behind my eyes this morning. I feel so incredibly sad.

I muster up the strength to put yesterday's yoga pants on that are laying on the old grey carpet in front of my closet. I put on the shirt that is laying on top of them and the socks from yesterday, put my hair in a ponytail, and splash my face with water. I eat a protein bar while I put on my jacket and UGGs and slip into the car.

I try to think good thoughts as I drive down the grid road and look at the huge sky and stare at the lonely moon. When I get to the clinic, I sit down in my familiar black chair, hold onto my cushion and try to start the routine for the first part of my session. I'm supposed to think positive thoughts, but today those positive thoughts just don't come.

It's much easier to think negatively than positively. Why does the worst case scenario always come to mind first? When violent harm thoughts pop into my brain, I'm supposed to be trained to say, "You have no power over me. I am in control." Sometimes I can do that and sometimes I can't. When I am unable to stop them, they start to cycle, leading to more negative thoughts: *This will never go away. I am stuck with this. I will always be like this.* The thoughts continue to lash at me. I picture someone getting kicked in the head, another person being stabbed with scissors or knives, and others being choked all around me. I try to keep going, to say, "I'm powerful! I am in control!" but eventually I resort to my old coping method. I turn the violence on myself. I slice my own wrists, stab myself, shove a knife into my brain until it stops.

It's hard to get out of the loop once it starts. It's hard not to feel sad and want to crawl under the covers and pray to make it stop. It's hard when you've been thinking you are doing better, only to fall back into your own traps. It feels like defeat but I know I'm only in the middle of my marathon. I know when people start running past me and it's getting harder and harder to breathe, that I should keep going. But let's face it – I'm not a runner and I've never won a race.

It's easier for me to be busy than alone with my thoughts. When my brain is quiet is when it's the worst. Apparently my brain doesn't like the quiet, it doesn't like meditation or the feeling of calm. It likes to be constantly firing endless rounds of bullets, it seems. When I feel my best is actually when stress takes over. When my cortisol is pumping and the adrenaline keeps me moving, my terrible thoughts don't have a chance to edge their way in. Whenever I start to feel a little bit better, I like to pile on some kind of responsibilities or activities because it is easier for me. If I keep my thoughts really busy with to-do lists and organizing, work and activities, I find relief up to a point. But then I reach that point, and my brain can't take it. I get overwhelmed by all the tasks that I took on and then I fall down an even darker hole. It's a cycle I know very well.

Transcranial magnetic stimulation (TMS) is supposed to move my cyclical, stuck-in-one-spot thoughts to other, more logical parts of my brain where they can be processed. Garbage! The new pathways are supposed to give the thoughts an easier route out, but I am discouraged at the lack of progress I have made. Not to mention if it ever does establish those new pathways, I will have to maintain those routes with self-care, therapy, SSRI meds, etc. until I die.

****

I continue to berate myself in the second session. I read my script for my Harm OCD thoughts and it sounds spot on for how I feel. The script consists of all the different ways I can harm myself …, "Beat her!" I think, "Just beat her."

I have always tried not to feel sorry for myself but when I get really low, like I feel today, I can't help to wonder what it must be like to just feel normal. To some people on the outside, my life could be considered a fairy tale:

She comes from a nice home with kind parents. Her siblings and extended family love to be together and have fun. She had pretty much straight A's in school, was never really in any trouble, got her degree, got her accounting professional designation, got her king, has two lovely princesses and one little prince, they have a little kingdom with grain and animals, a little castle, and the queen has always looked joyful and happy.

However, this fairy tale has a sick queen, and she struggles so hard with the demons in her mind that most days she wants to run from the kingdom. Where she would run, she doesn't know, but she wishes she could find peace.

If I were watching this queen, I would think, "What the hell is your problem? You have it all, you sad, mopey piece of trash. Aw, poor you."

Isn't that what everyone did to the Duchess of Sussex when she was having a hard time? How do we get to judge who has it easy and who has it hard?

Maybe I am sorry for myself because I feel powerless…powerless against my diseases, powerless about our world issues, powerless in the face of our politics… Nothing seems to fit. I certainly don't feel like I fit in anywhere.

But you don't want to hear my sad story, do you? You want me to talk about resilience, rising above, being an inspiration, being strong, brave, courageous, and giving you hope. The truth is that I can't give you hope; only you can give you hope. I can't give you inspiration; you need to be inspired. I can't make you be brave and courageous. Maybe just for today you could do that for me? You be the brave one, I'll be the weak one. You be the courageous one, I'll be the frightened one. You be the hope, I'll be the mope, and hopefully tomorrow we can switch.

TMS Session 19

I am still in a sad, bitter mood as I sit down today for therapy. I get stuck sometimes thinking that the TMS therapy and meds work for a while and then they just dump me, like a girlfriend who didn't get a card for Valentine's Day. I feel dumped. My own brain refuses to give me even a little card! Never mind the roses and fireworks, but just give me a damn card!

It's hard to keep going every day when you have these setbacks. I feel like I want to give up, and I tell myself it's not working. I just want to go home, crawl under the covers, and fall asleep, so that maybe when I wake up a re-set will happen, and I will be happy. Being sad is so fucking exhausting.

Today in the first part of the session where I think positive thoughts, I try to think of happy memories with my mother in law. She was a kind, gentle soul and I loved her dearly. She always gave me so much grace and helped me navigate the world of men, and her son in particular. One day we were standing outside on the farm, and she lit up a cigarette. She had been trying to quit on and off for years.

She looked over at me in tears and said, "I want to live. I want to be here for my grandchildren and children, but I just can't stop doing this. Why? I'm going to die, but I can't quit."

I wanted so badly to make her feel better. I looked at her and said, "You can't help it! Smoking is an addiction, just like alcohol, drugs, or in my case overeating. Even though I hate being fat, I can't stop stuffing my mouth with food. Obesity will kill me one day, but I can't quit either!"

But she only shook her head, as if she knew that her death wasn't that far off. And we did, in fact, lose her a few years later from emphysema and lung disease.

She was so ashamed when she started getting sicker, and didn't tell anyone about her illness until she was already on oxygen. By then it was too late. I can't understand how she could think that we wouldn't all love and support her until the end. Did she think we were going to say, "How stupid are you? What a stupid choice! I can't believe you chose cigarettes over us and your grandchildren you loved so dearly!"

Of course we wouldn't do that to her. We loved her too much for that.

Okay that was a strike out for positive thoughts in the first session. I tell myself this will never work if I have no happy thoughts to disperse around my head.

****

In the second session, I think about the judgement I have against myself and society's judgement against me and others with illnesses.

I have said that I need self-forgiveness to stop being so hard on myself, and it is on my to-do list! I know I have a disease, but sometimes because it is so invisible, it is hard to forgive. And while the treatments are becoming physically easier, emotionally they are still difficult. But I know I have made progress even though I have bad days. I've come a long way, made many connections, and realized what I need to do to care for myself. It seems easy enough – forgive yourself for having an invisible disease and the healing will begin!

I think of how some people I talk to say things like, "Good for you for getting treatment for this! Most people would be too ashamed of themselves." Huh? I have many types of diseases, both physical and mental. Why should my OCD and depression make me ashamed of myself, but not my endometriosis and ischemic colitis? Are physical illnesses less shameful? I am responsible for taking care of myself and for treating my diseases, but in the case of my mental illness, why am I commended for not being too ashamed of myself to get treatment! Whoah, ouch!

I think about someone who tried to commit suicide but didn't die. They had been addicted to some drug and eventually decided to try to kill themselves. Afterwards the family said, "What a stupid person! What a shame they ruined their life. For goodness sake, we all have problems. What were they thinking? How sad they had to ruin their life like that!" The family speaks of their loved one like this and then essentially goes on with their life, unable to forgive the person for making such a terrible decision. How is it that if they had a physical accident, like if they cut into their leg with a chainsaw, you wouldn't disown them, but if they have a substance abuse problem and are depressed to the point of suicide, then it's their fault?

None of these illnesses or accidents are anyone's fault. Of course there are ways to help, but those who don't get help and who lose the battle shouldn't require forgiveness. If your arteries are clogged, should you be ashamed? Do I need to forgive someone for having a heart attack? Do I need to forgive someone who had a brain aneurysm?

When does the stigma end that we make a choice to be an addict or a choice to commit suicide? It's a disease that may or may not respond to treatment, period, full stop. Maybe if I can recognize this in others then I can use that same line of thinking to forgive my own mental illness. How can I be ashamed of it and love myself at the same time?

TMS Session 20

Today I feel sarcastic and a bit like fighting back against my negativity in a snide way. As I sit down to think of positive thoughts in the first TMS session, I start to think of everything a person should do to be healthy. I write them down when I get home. It is an exhausting list.

-Have you drunk at least eight glasses of water today? Your body needs water every day to function.

-Did you exercise? You have to at least walk or do something once a day.

-How about fresh air? You need to breathe some fresh air.

-Have you been sitting too long? Too much sitting is dangerous to your health.

-Did you brush and floss your teeth? Dental hygiene is very important.

-Did you take your vitamins, medications, etc.? You don't want to get sick, you know.

-Did you eat healthy today? Did you have vegetables and fruit? You are what you eat.

-Did you wash your face and use 12 face creams? Your skin is very important, one day you will look like a wrinkly old bag.

-Did you limit your caffeine intake? You know it's bad for you – too much and you get anxious.

-Did you write in your gratitude journal today? If you have gratitude, you won't be so negative.

-Did you watch the budget today, and not spend too much on things you don't need? You are just throwing money out the window if you are buying coffee and things like that.

-Did you throw away something today? Your house is going to be full of clutter. Just throw away one thing per day and you will live so much cleaner.

-Did you make your bed? A made bed is the sign of an organized mind.

-Did you recycle? Recycling is very important, you want to save the earth, right?

-Did you put away some money in savings? You will need RRSPs and savings for the future.

-Did you put money away for your children's education? Very important, you are going to need five times what you needed when you went to school.

-Did you write down what you ate today so you know you didn't eat too many calories? Tomorrow when you feel fat, you will regret it.

-Did you respond back to all your messages promptly? You know you should always get back to people within a few hours.

-Did you do something for self-care today? Did you meditate and do deep breathing?

Did you do this list as well for every person in your household, pay the bills, go to work, volunteer, grocery shop, do the laundry, go to your kids sports, sign their forms, do their homework with them and for God's sake could you be a bit more positive? People are going to think you are always negative.

I want to make a new to-do list, because that one sounds too exhausting.

Michelle's checklist of items she accomplished today:

Did you tell anyone to piss off today? You didn't? Okay good job! Check list complete.

****

In the second part of my TMS session today I read my script and plan to address some of my nagging thoughts on death. I have discovered from some of my reading that this can also be an OCD theme just like harm, and it can ruminate over and over in your thoughts. When you have anxiety or OCD, you have a fear of uncertainties. Even though I feel better now than when this journey began, I ultimately still am perplexed by death and its uncertainty. I remember talking to my therapist about this years ago. I described to him how my mind sometimes gets stuck on the idea of "forever" and how it can be and when it ends. I would often get stuck on this theme when I was in bed and trying to go to sleep, and it would become an endless loop.

At the time he had said, "What does it matter? When your life is over and you no longer exist, then there is nothing left to worry about, because you won't be there any longer."

This was not helpful for me because that thought always throws me for a loop. How could my brain, my narrator, my soul, no longer exist, and why? What would be the purpose of it all? Why would we be here just to die?

Everything about life is uncertain and the ultimate uncertainty is what happens when we die. I really don't understand any of it, but there are certain things that are more perplexing to me. Why do young people and children die? Why do young mothers and fathers die? If you love someone deeply, is life ever really long enough? You read about wars from the past and the millions of men who died fighting, and for what purpose? I mean I understand why people would have died fighting against Hitler, or fighting for a cause they believed in or if their freedom was at stake, but when you die fighting to conquer another land, what is to gain from that? Where do they go, those millions and millions of souls that have died over humanity's time on earth?

This makes me think about another thing I find puzzling. Some people say that life didn't mean much in the distant past. But why wouldn't it? Even back then, people were human beings with brains and souls, so how could they not have pondered staying safe and striving to live as long as they could? What makes us different now?

I guess if all you knew from birth was just survival, and everyone died around you all the time, it would just be something normal. Is it possible that when their mother or father died, their little sister or brother, people in the past cried for a few minutes and then just carried on, knowing they didn't have much time either? Does knowing that you should have more time make it harder to accept dying? I think it's possible that knowing that we live in a warm safe place with wonderful connections to family and friends and with a life expectancy of around 80 years makes us cherish our life that much more.

I sometimes wonder if because everything is so much more precious to us that our minds can't take it. It's just too stressful to know that if you don't cherish every snowflake and video, every one of your baby's moves that you will somehow miss it and it will be gone forever? Does our longer life span make us worry that we won't enjoy life enough?

I asked my 90-year-old Dad what was the best time period to live in. I wanted him to say the 1950s, when life was simple, there was no war, and there was no internet and knowing a million things that happened in the world. He did say that it was great back then, but he was also quick to add that it's hard to say what is better or what is worse because they didn't know back then that one day they would be able to travel to Australia on a plane, enjoy a beach vacation in Hawaii, have access to the weather on the iPad, talk to their children with facetime in Paris. He basically said that every time period has been great in its own way. We have so many more ways of saving lives now, more medicines when we are ill, more technology so he can watch the curling games broadcast from Nova Scotia. It is all so wonderful. Does it have a downside? Sure it does, just like the downside in the 1950s was that they didn't have lifesaving drugs and techniques to help them live longer. But they also didn't have all the media constantly thrown at them. They didn't have a choice to travel, see the world, do all the great things we do today, but it also didn't bother them because they never knew that it existed or that it was something that they desired. You can't desire something that doesn't exist.

    It's really about perspective. My dad's perspective is to enjoy what you have when you have it, and to not look around wondering why or how it could be better or worse. Really it is up to all of us to take the good and filter out the bad, to take what serves us emotionally, physically and spiritually, and filter out what does not enhance our quality of life. How profound is it that we get the choice to do that when others in the past never had that possibility? They fought for survival and had no other way.

    I guess the real question is what do you want to do with all you have been given? How do we live so we get the best out of all of our blessings? For me, I'm going to stop feeling like I have to make the most of every minute. I will no longer feel guilty if I don't make every moment magical. I want to sit in the hot tub like I did this morning with the snow falling on my nose and feel pure bliss for an ordinary snowstorm day. I want to be thankful that I have a TV to stream any types of programming I want to watch. I want to embrace mediocrity and the peace that comes with it.

    For the last few weeks, I have been trying to live a more peaceful life. I've played lots of games with my husband and kids, I've watched stimulating programming, I've done yoga, I've sat writing in front of a fire, and I've made muffins with my little guy. I turned down the rush factor of everything, and I want more of it. Life with more quiet and less rush has been deeply satisfying. I couldn't sit still about a month ago, my brain was firing all over the place and at all times. I felt like it wouldn't even let me breathe. Through all the treatment, hard work, and stillness I have experienced, it has finally started to rest.

    Part of my mind resting is coming to terms with my fear of death and my constant questioning about the uncertainty that surrounds it. So this is my peaceful thought to put this to rest tonight. No matter what happens when we die, I hope we are at peace. I hope that we are deeply satisfied that the choices we have made have led us to a purpose that empowers our soul to release with gratitude at a life not magically lived with how much money or faraway lands we have seen but to release with love of a life that gave us love and comfort in between its storms and that it is ready to move on to whatever its next step maybe. The cocoon has no way of knowing that it is soon to be turning into a butterfly. Possibly the best is yet to come.

TMS Session 21

I'm still feeling like sarcastically lashing out by making funny lists. Today during the first session, I thought of things that annoy me but make me laugh.

-Taking grocery bags into the grocery store. How can I remember that shit every single time? Also, I probably have like 500 now, so am I really saving the environment?

-Paper straws. They suck. No pun intended.

-That I can fit into a medium, large, x-large and xx-large. Can clothing manufacturers just get their shit together?

-Climate tax payments, GST and other payments the government gives us in return for us paying them. Screw off! Just make the payment what you want it to be, and we will all pay it, and you won't need 1,242 people working out the numbers and mailing out the cheques.

-Cereal that doesn't come in ziplock bags.

-Why fruits and vegetables are so expensive.

-You are supposed to fold fitted sheets.

-Tik Tok, such addictive shit.

-When it's sunny when you go to work and rainy and cold on the weekend.

-When every software thing needs an update on like ten different devices.

-All the passwords we need, forgetting your password, getting locked out of something, getting an email, getting back in, making a new password with the wrong amount of digits, making it again without a special character, making it again but forgetting to whirl around three times and say the magic word before it will be accepted.

-When things freeze at the back of the fridge.

-When you buy six bags of pancake mix because someone keeps saying you are out of pancake mix and putting it in a different location each time.

-Grocery carts that require change that you don't have in your wallet, in the car, in your console or in your shoe.

-When you take antibiotics to fix something and then you end up still sick AND you have a yeast infection.

-People that bring kids who have just finished throwing up two hours ago to special events.

-Cats running in the garage every time the door opens, then hiding so you have to get a broom and run around and yell like a pig squealing to get them out of the garage, then just as the garage door almost hits the ground, they run back in again and the cycle continues until you just quit and let them defecate in the garage.

-When you are walking down the road, and a garter snake scares the shit out of you and slithers right in front of your shoe.

-When you order groceries online and you ask for long grain rice and they substitute minute rice. If I wanted minute rice, I would have bought minute rice!!

-When you get your nails done for an event and you break one so now you just end up looking like a clown with nine big nails and one short ripped off one.

-When you are in a shower at a campsite and they have motion lights on the other side of the building and no one else is there and you are the only one in the bathroom, so you shower in the dark and then slip on the cement and cut your leg shaving.

-When you start laughing so hard you pee your pants a little bit but don't know if anyone can see and are wondering how long it will take until someone can smell it, because you aren't at home and you didn't bring along a second pair of underwear like you are in potty training.

-When you have thrown up so much all you have is bile left and you yell out into the toilet like an elephant giving birth.

-When you burn the soup on the bottom of the pan.

-When you can't pass a vehicle and it's driving 50 km/hr and you yell out, "Hey! Are you hauling around eggs or what?" and you really badly want to give them the finger but your kids are in the car and also as you drive by you realize they are 85 and half blind and probably shouldn't drive faster than 50 km/hr.

-When the power goes out and all you have in the fridge is cold lasagna to warm up in the microwave and you actually go through a checklist of like 25 things that you can't eat or do, before you just settle with the candle and the peanut butter sandwich and check X to see how long this misery will last.

-When you are in the pool and someone tells you that you have snot on your upper lip.

-When you go to the wrong grocery store line, and Cindy from the check out has to call housewares to see how much the fork is that someone is trying to buy, and they are insisting the fork is on sale.

-When your food is way too hot, but you are really hungry, and the roof of your mouth takes another skinning with the mozzarella cheese from the pizza and even though it burns you still keep doing it because you are that hungry.

-When you trip walking up stairs and then you mumble to yourself and laugh but no one is laughing around you, they are just embarrassed for you.

-When you saved yourself the last piece of pie and you go to the fridge excitedly because you have been waiting all day and someone else ate it.

****

I'm still feeling cheeky as I head into my second session and read my script. As I continue laughing in my head about the sarcastic list of things that annoy me, my script is harder and harder to read. It's just not sticking in my head. I start thinking of a conversation my husband Kevin and I had this past weekend, and want to see if I could sort some of it out in my session.

Yesterday we were driving to a lake about forty minutes from our house. We passed a large new house being built, and as I usually do and have always done in the last thirty years, I said, "Oh look! There's my dream house!"

I waited for Kevin's response, expecting his usual, "Yeah I bet they have a lot of money," or "Wow! Could you set your sights any higher?"

But he surprised me with a different response. He said, "Would you trade all of the trips we have had over the last thirty years for that house?"

In my mind, I immediately thought, "Absolutely not. I would never trade all those amazing memories for a house."

But aloud I stuck to being spoiled Michelle and said with a grin, "Why can't I have both?"

He shook his head as usual. I could have left it at that. Then it would have ended like a thousand of our other conversations. He would have said, "You need to have a goal and make a budget if you want to live like that," and I would have said, "Well I can't help it if I want to have nice things." Then I would have retreated back into myself, feeling like shit that the 12-year-old girl in me who never got her castle. . But instead, I said something totally different. I looked over at him and said, "You know I wouldn't have changed a thing. Yes you are correct - if it had been something that I wanted more than anything else, I would have made different decisions, and would have worked and saved differently."

I have realized that it was all within my power to make different choices. But the truth is that I didn't, and I absolutely don't regret it. Maybe the big beautiful house will still come one day, and maybe it won't. But if it doesn't, I am absolutely good with knowing that even though that looked like my dream life from a young age, the truth is that I loved to travel more than I realized, and my choices in life reflect that.

My auntie lived in a small little post office house in a little nowhere broken down town. She lost her husband at a young age – I believe he was in his fifties. She loved Hawaii, and they travelled there many, many times. She had little pill boxes of sand from the beaches she had gone to on shelving in her little kitchen. Her kitchen didn't have a sink. To wash dishes, she had to go to the back porch and fill up a bucket of hot water, add the bubbly soap and bring it back to the kitchen counter to wash the cups and plates from her morning coffee. She had coffee every day with her brothers mostly, and sometimes in laws, sometimes nieces like me when it was a day off school. I still remember all the food she used to make for us. She would make donuts that you could dip in her sugar bowl, and Nanaimo squares that tasted like yellow candied brownies. She would have crackers, sausage, cheese, sometimes cinnamon buns, sometimes other sweet treasures. She would serve the piping hot coffee in the Corelle white mugs with the green flowers on the top. Then she would continually keep filling up the cup, even when you weren't looking, because she always wanted you to stay a little longer.

The talk around the table was which field the brothers were growing wheat on, how dry that summer has been, what the relatives in BC were doing, and any mention of trips to be taken. I would look up from the table and see the sand in the small clear bottles all lined up and think about the memories that she stored in those little vials.

I remember one time when I was a bit older and she was living in another small house in a bigger centre, we started talking about vacations. She walked over to a cedar chest and pulled out a long piece of paper and showed it to me. The paper detailed all the trips she had been on, how many times she had been to Hawaii with my uncle and then after he passed, and how many times they went to Hungary to visit my uncle's homeland.

That piece of paper was her most precious possession. It indeed had cost a lot more money than the tiny little modest houses that she lived in, but it represented all her dreams and joy, and documented a life well lived. Just a small town girl who got to see the world, she experienced more than she ever imagined possible as a prairie farm girl born in the 1920s.

She has now lost her memory to Alzheimer's, but I swear if I could ask her whether she would trade a big house for that scrap piece of paper full of memories, hands down she would say that she didn't regret a thing.

I've always had a love of travelling and seeing what the world had to offer. When we went to the lake this weekend to stay at a friend's cabin, my son Brant was ecstatic to go. He loves every hotel, every road trip, every canoe trip down our backroad. He loves to see the world. Kevin laughs and says, "He is just like you in so many ways! He always wants to be anywhere but home."

I ponder that statement as it comes out of Kevin's mouth. Do I always want to be anywhere but home? Do I not like home so much that I am just never happy? I catch myself before I start to give myself a tongue lashing about never being happy. I have learned so much in the last couple months about being kinder to myself that I just ponder the statement and its truth instead.

I have come to the conclusion that just because I always like to travel and be somewhere else, it doesn't mean that I am not happy here in my home. In fact, it can be quite the opposite. I can be very happy in my comfortable home! I can love coming back here every time I leave, but that doesn't mean that I need to take away my love of travel.

I love seeing the world from every different perspective. I love to see its North Rock, its crystal-clear cold lakes, and its stunning miles and miles of never-ending evergreens. I loved seeing the east coast with its lighthouses and having the sun beam on us in a wooden ship that smelled like the early 1900s, when our ancestors arrived in this amazing country. I love the stories of years past, and how they arrived here to board a train to an unknown harsh terrain. I loved seeing our nation's capital and sitting in where all the greatest decisions for our society our made. I loved Niagara Falls, the wondrous rushing water, and the view from the stunning CN tower. I fell in love as a child with Casa Loma, the castle and the stories of the tunnels to the stables.

Then there are the prairies, where ordinary days are ended with extraordinary sunsets, when the sky turns orange, red, and purple, and the clouds make designs that a painter could never even dream of painting. The seasons change and you get to enjoy the first buds coming on the trees, the smell of the spring rain, the green grass and the heat of summer, the colors of autumn, the warmth of a cozy blanket and a cup of tea while you sit in front of a fire looking out at the blowing snow, and every day is one more step to another season.

Onward to the West Coast where the most exquisite places on earth exist – the mountains, the lakes the color of teal diamonds…if you mixed blue and green paint together you could never come up with a color so incredibly beautiful. In Vancouver you see the wondrous ocean again, nestled in front of the mountain tops. You can taste the ocean breeze on the ferry. It is a mix of sea salt with a hint of fish, with evergreen and rock mixed in…no candle imaginable could compare with that smell that you can feel in your soul all the way to your toes.

Oh my gosh! I haven't even left Canada yet, and there are so many other places we have been! I could write for hours of the wondrous world that we live in. Now I ask again: would you trade any of those things for where you sleep at night? Big or small, high ceiling or low, room to dance or room to squeeze by, windows that face the west or that face a tractor?

Do you find something new about every single day? Do you feel the soul of the ancestors that came before you, the higher power that you know had to have created the colors and the wonders of our amazing world? Do you try to do the hula dance with a stranger, do you taste a curry made by a street vendor, do you jump in the ocean and feel the salt and silk on your skin, do you climb a mountain, do you share a laugh with strangers on an airplane, do you see your children's eyes when they are snorkeling and see a turtle, do you see all the things, smell all the different smells, feel all the things that are possible to feel?

  It transports us to view the world from someone else's perspective and we are forever changed. Every new experience fills us deeper and deeper, more than a bricks and mortar ever could do. I don't feel bad that my soul likes to fly. It was meant to soar. No earthly possessions could be traded for its wonder.

  I don't feel bad that my soul likes to fly. It was meant to soar. I would not trade its wonder for any earthly possession.

TMS Session 22

As I sit down at TMS today to focus on my positive thoughts, I think about the list of annoyances I made yesterday and how good it felt to laugh at them.

There were many times when the kids were little that I would make up silly stories about two geese, Fred and Elsie or whatever names I felt like at the time. I would act out how they were having an argument, and Elsie was mad that Fred had been looking at other geese, or something else silly like that. The kids would laugh and laugh and add their own parts onto the story. I still love to make up stories of what animals are thinking. I would also do funny sounding voices with all kinds of things that end with "says Bear." There were always lots of giggles. In fact, the kids thought that instead of a chartered accountant I should have been one of The Wiggles! I would always laugh and say, "That would have been my dream job, just to act like a clown all day and get paid for it!"

I think in many ways I created those little worlds for them so I could have a break from being the dark depressive OCD me. It seems strange that people who are always trying to make others laugh are the ones that are really sad on the inside. Why is that? Is it because we are hiding and showing a different persona of ourselves, or is it truly relieving just to be funny for a few minutes? Probably a little bit of both, but I wouldn't want to give it up for a second. Laughing at some of the things I wrote yesterday brought me to tears when I read them to my daughter last night.

Since my mind has been starting to clear there are a few things that I have noticed. I have a longer attention span with movies and shows. I don't feel as forgetful, but feel more casually planned out. I definitely feel less stress, less guilt, less harshness towards the choices I make. I'm treating myself more like a friend, and I am happy for me that I get to relish life in this space, where the mean, self-criticizing voice is not totally gone, but it is manageable. I am able to overcome it by saying things like, "It's alright, everyone makes mistakes. No big deal, this will be okay." My anxieties about "what-ifs" are also starting to lessen.

I have installed an app on my phone that helps with my OCD. The exercises there are really helping me with understanding positive things to embrace and negative things to trash. Things I didn't even know I had a problem with before all of this are getting resolved. Every day the exercises bring out something more in me that I never knew I could actually have control over. For example, here are just some of the things I've realized:

    I can calm myself down. (Oh my gosh who knew? I really can calm myself down!)

    I can decide to overcome my fear. (What? It always controlled me!)

    Not all negative events are catastrophes. (Really? When there are 22 plastic wrappers of fruit snacks under Brant's bed, it isn't a catastrophe? I can actually just clean it up and address it?)

    I can stop monitoring my body when I decide to. (Again, really? This is my choice??)

    In most cases, my attention is mostly under my control. (Seriously? I can tell myself to be more attentive?)

    Feeling uncertain is a natural part of life. (You mean everyone is dealing with uncertainty, everywhere?)

    I know this all may seem like regular common sense to most people, but it isn't to me. It is actually mind blowing, and not in a sarcastic way, either. I have lived under the depression umbrella for so long that I didn't know choices even existed. I'm sure at some points in my life I did have control, but I haven't felt it in so long that I don't even remember it.

    One recent event has shown me my progress. For months, I have been scared to go back to doing meditation. The last few times I did it, which was several months ago, my negative violent thoughts were out of control, and I couldn't sit with myself. This morning, I was on YouTube and chose a yoga class to do for mental health. I didn't mean to pick a meditation video, but I accidentally started one, so I decided to finish.

    Probably about three minutes in, the violent thoughts started. I saw someone coming behind me and slitting my throat. I didn't actually see who they were, or anything else about them. All I saw was the knife coming towards my throat, stabbing my neck, as blood comes spurting out. My first thought after was, "Oh no, not again! Here we go, I'll never make it through this meditation." But right after that thought, I said, "NO! This is not happening! I am taking control of this. It has no power over me. If I stop it from creeping up on me, I will stop the cycle." It came back one more time and again I was emphatic with my "NO." After that, I was able to complete the rest of the 20 minute meditation! Controlling this is a major achievement for me.

Before going through all of this, I knew the violent thoughts were a problem, but I had no idea what the depression had done to me for so long. It's like if there is a lake, but there's a mountain blocking it…how would you know the lake is there? I didn't know the lake was there. I didn't know that I had the power to take out my map and see the entire landscape. In fact, I didn't even know there was a map! All I saw was the mountain…big, tall, made of hard rock that I could never or would never crawl over. But once I found the map, and saw the lake, I knew I wanted to get to it. It was a difficult journey and one that I didn't know at times if I would make it but I am glad I kept following the map.

I think we all have a map. Yours might look different than mine, but there is definitely a map. If you are struggling, the one gift I can give you is to promise that there is a lake behind the mountain. There are many different ways of getting there – bus, taxi, jeep, bicycle, train – and you have to try them all to see which one takes you there. But don't give up.

****

This afternoon I'm going to get some headshot pictures done. I have been thinking about what to wear every day for the last ten days, but haven't tried anything on or even taken the time to look at my clothes. I think what's weighing on me is that I am afraid I won't like the way I look in anything, so I have been avoiding it. This morning, I tried on some outfits and got my daughters Ava and Kierra, along with Kevin, to judge which one was best. I have this picture of myself in my mind that I want to look like. I don't look like her though. My face is chubby and I have fat chin jowls. I tried to use cold water and a freezer facial tool to bring down my puffiness, but it didn't help. Even my nose looks like a big honker when I'm puffy. I decided to eat no salt until after the pictures at 1:00 p.m. However, I knew I needed fluid, so I grabbed a couple of waters and a Powerade. As I was drinking the Powerade, I thought, "How stupid I am! This has salts in it to hydrate me, and now it is going to make my face even fuller!"

My thoughts took over. "Why can't I even get this right? How is it I can't even keep my face from looking fatter than it already does?" My anxiety was so high that morning that I only allowed myself a little bit of coffee. I was on edge and I knew it.

Ava tried to calm me down as she worked on my make up. I kept telling her to make shadows under my chin on either side, to make it appear that I have a jawline.

Finally, she exclaimed, "Mom, stop this! You need to like your own face!"

"I can't right now! Just do your best on the makeup and maybe the pictures will turn out well."

I had the first few pictures taken with my suit jacket on, because that's what I wanted to look like. When I saw the first images on screen, they were awful. The suit jacket made me look way bigger and my face looked horrible. I didn't even recognize the person on the screen. Really, I can't possibly be that fat! When I take selfies and I hold the phone three feet above my head, I don't look like that! Apparently this habit has given me a false sense of how I look. But now the pictures right there on the screen told me the truth. That is not what I want to look like. The pictures disgusted me.

I changed clothes and it helped a little. When we went through the pictures again, I saw a few that were okay to me, and Kevin really liked them. He said they were great, and that I looked awesome. I looked at him and wondered what he saw. Does he like this person with this fat face? Has he forgotten after all these years that he usually was attracted to thinner women, unlike myself? He tries all kinds of tactics to make me feel better about myself, like saying, "Your jeans look so good on you! You look beautiful!" None of it works and I think how could I be surprised I am upset with these pictures. How could I not expect the fat faced girl, like she lost 10 pounds off her face last night.

Have I fooled myself into thinking that I look better than I actually do? Why does the woman in the pictures, who has an obese BMI and does in fact have a fat face, surprise and mortify me? Do I think that somehow overnight I got my 140-pound face back, and that the pictures would melt the rest away and I would look like the person that I want to be?

When we got home, I overheard Ava asking Kevin why I get like this.

"I think since she had her breakdown she has lost a lot of confidence," he tells her.

Is that why? Maybe when I told my family, friends and co-workers about my real mental health struggles I blew my façade wide open. Now I've stripped away a layer of protection that I don't know how to cover back up. Yes, I want to cover it, it doesn't feel natural to say I am good just the way that I am. I want to be somebody else, somebody who doesn't have these illnesses and someone who likes her fat face.

How do I accept myself as I am? I've talked about forgiveness, and I think I have forgiven myself for my ailments, but what lies beneath? Where do I get acceptance of this person? Why do I need to think I look pretty in these photos? And why does it have to be a version of pretty that no longer exists? The image I have of myself is an earlier version of me, someone I used to be. I need to look myself square in the eyes and say, "I am 48 years old, and this is the face I have."

Why do I need to be pretty, and pretend I am 20 years old? My husband, family and friends love me the way that I am. It wouldn't even matter to them if I grew a big wart on my nose! Although you better believe I'd be at the doctor as fast as I could, getting that thing removed! But they would still love me, even with the wart!

At least I think they would... Come to think of it, maybe Kevin wouldn't. The truth is, he would be disgusted by the wart. He has strong ideals of beauty and what looks good and what doesn't. He is constantly saying that he knows style, that he knows better than me what looks good. He's always saying he needs to take a couple of pounds off his stomach, then when he does, he struts around like a rooster who could get any peacock he wanted.

When I write to figure out an issue, I don't ever want to blame anyone for anything. But I have to look at this honestly. Has my worry about my appearance developed because of Kevin's own appearance insecurities? Have I attached his perfect form of beauty to mine? Don't get me wrong you know I always was like this long before I met Kevin in childhood and teenager. However, has it perpetuated that I be like him because I love him and that's what he wants? He says I have it though, he says it all the time, I guess though just like doubting the tms therapy, does he really mean it this time? Also, I know that it has to come from me in order to believe it. People can influence your perceptions but ultimately it is your choice what you believe about yourself.

I'm watching myself and I'm sitting on a teeter totter, where the person that sinks to the ground is heavier and the person on the other side is lighter. The lighter one gets to feel the ride, she gets to see things from a higher perspective, she gets to have fun, she gets to giggle. The heavy one sinks to the ground and can't even bring up the momentum to let the light one come down to the ground so she can have a ride. She sits there trying to push her legs against the ground, but she goes nowhere. She is too heavy for the other person, and no matter how hard she tries she will never make it into the air.

What if she realized that the person on the other side of the teeter totter wasn't someone she needed to be partnered with? What if she realized that maybe the teeter totter wasn't for her and the light girl to play on, because they weren't a match? What if instead of the teeter totter she went over to the slide, used her muscles to climb to the top, breathed in the air from up high with a smile on her face and then slid down with a giggle?

I think that's it, I think she has to get the hell off the teeter totter and go find the slide. How do I show her where the slide is? How do I show her that it isn't any use sitting at the bottom of the teeter totter trying to get to the top, because this teeter totter isn't for her? How do I make her happy that she still can go on the slide? I guess I have to make her believe that the slide is just as fun but it's different. She's different.

I see her in the headshot now and she is smiling. She looks at the picture and she says, "Yep, that's me. That feels like me, that looks like me." She is 48 years old and she is pretty enough. She's pretty enough to be exactly where she is in life. She is so much more than her weight – she is strong and she wants to help others in their own mental health journey. She wants everyone to enjoy life. She wants to play games and laugh by the campfire. She is the one who others talk about, saying, "I would like to be like her, not because she is pretty, but because she is kind, thoughtful, fun, accepting, and loves others so deeply that she can feel their own pain in her soul."

The thing that she wants for them is peace and a love-filled journey. That is more important than having a beautiful headshot.

TMS Session 23

I'm over halfway through my sessions, and all I can think when I sit down to get my magnet helmet strapped on my head is how up and down, back and forth like a see-saw this has all been. Sometimes I feel okay, like when I was laughing about some of those old stories I was writing about. Today I start to think of more of them.

While I am the child of farmers, I never did chores or drove a tractor or anything like that until I married Kevin. One time he left for a few days with his mom to help her buy a new van, and I was in charge of the farm and the girls. As I stood looking out the window, I could see one of the cows in the field was in labor. I watched her and realized she wasn't moving, and seemed to have been in the same spot for way too long. I walked the short distance from the house to the pasture only to realize she was dead, and the calf was lying alive beside her. I went back to the house to make a bottle and I decided to put the girls in the car and drive back over to the pasture because I wasn't sure how long it would take, and I wanted to keep them with me. I started chasing this little calf with the bottle in my hand, trying to get it to suck, but it kept moving away from me. I tried harder and harder and eventually the calf pushed me off, and I fell into the after birth, poop and the hind end of the dead mother cow. EWWWWWW! I jumped up and before I got in the car, I quickly took off my sweat pants that were covered in poop and blood. I was frantically trying to close the barbed wire gate, but unfortunately, it had started to rain, and my hands kept slipping. Out of nowhere, I heard a truck drive up. It was the guy who rents land from us. There I was, with wet hair, in my underwear, trying to close the gate. I quickly ran back to the car and climbed inside.

He walked up, saying, "Whatcha doing?" and "Can I help you?"

I was dying of embarrassment, and in my head I said to him, "Please, and let us never speak of this again."

But somehow I also was happy I was wearing black undies and not some see-through tightie whities. Always a good idea to wear good underwear.

****

It doesn't take me long to go from the positives in the first session to read my script and think of negative things for the next session. All it takes is one little thing and I spiral down into sadness. It's hard to get back out when I get stuck. In my last book, *The Thoughts I See*, I explore why I sometimes feel like I hate myself. There are many possible explanations, but the most plausible is the depression itself. The one question I keep asking is, "Why do I feel stupid?" I got A's in school, B's in university, and passed my Chartered Accountant designation on the first try. At work I always have positive performance appraisals; on my last appraisal, which was during one of the hardest times of my life, I scored higher then I had in years.

I've tried to watch myself to figure out where it's coming from when I hear the I am so stupid voice in my head. I have begun to realize that it happens when I experience any type of negative reaction or rejection. No matter what it is about, I automatically feel stupid, even if it has nothing to do with me being stupid. Even just a little, "Why didn't I think of that?" sends me spiraling into thoughts of "How stupid you are!" The same thing happens when someone questions my judgement on anything. I immediately think, "How stupid do you think I am?" It's like an automatic defensive default.

Out of curiosity I looked up the term *to be on the defensive* and found these definitions. Merriam-Webster states: "in the state or condition of being prepared or required to defend against attack or criticism."

Vocabulary.com says that someone on the defensive is: *concerned with justifying their actions of words. They have a defensive attitude as they try to protect themselves. If you know that to defend is to protect, you have an idea what defensive means. When a person is acting defensive, they're trying to protect or justify themselves.*

Why do I need to protect and justify myself? Why do I need to prove that I'm not stupid?

When I think of others who are defensive, I usually think that it's because there is some truth to what is being said. The person gets overly defensive because they either don't see what they did was wrong or they don't want to admit that what they did was wrong. What I do is internalize the admission of wrongdoing by telling myself I'm stupid. Why can't I just accept the consequence that I may have overlooked something? Why don't I ever want to be wrong? Is it back to perfection, like you aren't perfect if you are wrong sometimes?

    I have always felt that when people don't show up for me with really poor excuses, they have rejected me, and it makes me feel stupid that I even asked them for their help in the first place. I have tried to organize some fun events over the years and so many have fallen flat because everyone was busy. In my university years, my friends began calling me "Rudy." Rudy was one of the contestants on the show *Survivor* at the time. He bossed (or organized) everyone. When things didn't go his way, he would get mad. My friends told me that they liked Rudy because he made things happen and got everyone together, but I always took it as a criticism. It made me see myself as being too pushy in trying to organize things and getting too upset when things didn't go my way.

    So, I'm sensitive I guess – sensitive to criticism, sensitive to rejection, all of the roads lead back to me, me, me, trying to get my self-worth from other people.

    How do I learn to get my self-worth from myself instead? Forgiveness, yes, but there has to be more. I have to live with me (the narrator in my brain) for 365 days a year, 16 hours a day, and I don't like her because she is sensitive. She's such a crybaby. I want to tell her, "Toughen up, loser. Not everything is about you. Are you such a narcissist that you think the world should revolve around you?"

    Why do others' doubts about me make me doubt myself? Why can't I be stronger than that? And why does it even matter what others think of me? In most cases I think people actually like me more than I like myself, but for some reason I keep requiring external validation to no end, and I can never get internal validation.

    I scan my mind for when I started to feel this way, and I just can't remember ever *not* feeling this way. I looked at photographs the other day from when I was about seven or eight years old, and I remember looking at them when they were first taken and pointing out which ones I looked fat in and which ones I thought I looked pretty in. I look at them now and I am so sad for that cute little girl. What could have made her internalize all that criticism? I honestly don't know. No one berated or shamed me at that young age. I mostly got love and adoration for being a perfect little girl. For whatever reason I felt that being the perfect little girl had to be done in my head as well, and I could never measure up to my own perfect image.

TMS Session 24

I continue on with my first session of TMS with thoughts of funny stories that I can remember, and I start thinking about potty training my children. I won't embarrass the kid who did this, but during the potty training for one of them, I remember that every time I came into the kitchen, the tea towel that hangs on the oven would be lying on the floor. I would think it odd and just pick it up and hang it right back up. But then one day as I was coming around the corner, I saw what was happening to the tea towel. The potty trainer was using it for toilet paper, like it was a feather boa at a strip club, then dropping it on the floor. EWWWWWW but how funny! That same kid also put her head in a toilet full of pee and toilet paper once just to get my attention.

All three of my kids were the type to get into trouble. Truthfully it was likely because I was always working on something or in the kitchen but there were so many messes. Diaper cream all over their faces, baby powder and lotion all over the rug, plants dug up, many, many bottles of shampoo and lotion poured in the bathtub or behind beds or in trucks. My makeup brushes were a favorite, as were my face creams. In at least two instances a whole jar of my face cream was used with a makeup brush to "paint" something with – one time it was my make up mirror and one time it was…socks…?? One time as I had a bath, I could hear my girls cleaning outside and singing a song about cleaning. I thought it was so cute! Cute until I got out of the tub and they had poured a whole bottle of dish soap all over the floor and were busy mopping bubbles everywhere. For those wondering, yes, I did get mad about these messes, but I also always had to laugh, take a picture and credit their creativity.

****

People want answers from me sometimes. *How did you get like this? When did it start? Why?* I want to say, "You tell me why!" I certainly didn't make up having these violent thoughts. They were an obsession resulting from my self hate. I have always thought they began during my university days, but recently I've wondered if they started before that. I knew that when I was younger, I was afraid of my uncle who had schizophrenia, and I remember seeing him in my mind killing Mom and Dad and me every night. Maybe these were the first obsessive violent thoughts, which would mean they started around age 10 or 11 – earlier than I had originally thought.

I remember one night when I was a child and a friend was having supper at our home. We were eating outside and all of a sudden my uncle either fired shots in the air or started hollering with a gun in his hand. She and I ran with our plates into the house. I was messaging with this same friend today, and I started to question what really happened that night. I asked her if she had any memory of it. Sure enough, she confirmed that she remembered it as well. She said she remembered being scared that he was going to come after us and hurt us. She said we ran in the house and at some point we called Dad and he went over to see what was going on. She remembered that we hid out upstairs. We were around 12 or 13 years old at the time. Honestly, I felt relieved that she remembered it the same way I did, and that I wasn't just making up some kind of extraordinary memories to prove where some of my deepest fears came from.

Even the nightmares that I continued to have throughout my whole life were running and hiding from someone trying to kill me. Could it have been so ingrained in my brain at a young age that it stuck in there and it played over and over on repeat? I think that maybe because I was genetically predisposed to OCD also contributed to it. Whenever I get stressed or hormonal, that fear of being chased comes back. Sometimes, when it is really severe, the violent thoughts center on my children. My mind's reaction to this is a compulsion to kill myself to stop the thoughts from happening. My children are my most precious possessions, and I would die to keep them safe from harm.

TMS Session 25

Today I continue on the theme of happy thoughts, focusing on stories of the kids. The things that happened with them growing up were sometimes so frustrating but sometimes it was so hard not to laugh.

Our little guy Brant liked to do things to get my attention. On one camping trip when he was about three years old, he was mad at me for something that went wrong with his hot dog. That night he poured relish all over my pillow and over the bottom sheet and then placed the comforter back over it, so I didn't see it until I was about to get into it! I was so upset that I told the girls they needed to put him to bed, because after I changed the sheets I was going to crawl underneath them and wonder what I did to deserve such nutty kids! That one I was too mad to take a picture of!

****

During my TMS treatment for OCD, I am supposed to keep my thoughts stuck in my normal pattern of obsessional thoughts, which is hard to do when the normal reaction is to cast these thoughts aside. My technician suggested I write a script to work myself up, to get my thoughts going and to keep them there so that when the magnets hit, they can move these thoughts to other more logical parts of my brain where my brain can go: *Huh? No way? That's awful!*

Today is day 25 out of 40, and as I am reading my script I think about how awful the things written there are. When I read it, I almost think someone else wrote it. I'm going to share it because I believe now that I am down to five of these experiences a day instead of 400 or 500. It's important to remember how far I have come. I also want to give hope to others that something so heinous in my brain can be helped through the right therapy and medication.

Script:

Every knife I see I slit my wrists, stab myself in the stomach, stab myself in the head.

I see voices taking over my head and making me do terrible things.

In response I stab myself.

I see voices telling me to hit a semi on the highway.

In response I stab myself.

I see me hanging myself.

In response I stab myself.

I see me overdosing.

In response I choke myself, slit my throat and stab myself.

See violent images of others getting violently hurt, stabbed, throats and faces slashed.

Stab myself.

Feel I've done something stupid.

Stab myself.

Feel I've upset someone.

Stab myself.

Feel I've done something wrong.

Stab myself.

See rope. Hang myself.

See cords, choke myself.

Why won't they stop?

I try to sleep, I just ignore the thoughts and they keep coming, slash my wrists, hold a gun in my mouth and pull the trigger, do it right, make sure it gets up in your brain, kill that brain.

Tell it to shut up, I can't stand listening to it, I close my eyes and it won't stop.

I don't trust myself sometimes, I want to run, run, run.

I'm so lazy, I have no energy, I'm so tired. Kill it, end it.

I hate everyone's expectations of me and my own. I'm drowning. Drown, under the water, drown.

I'm driving, someone is choking me from behind.

Someone grabs me from behind the shower curtain and slits my throat.

Someone walks up behind me sitting on the couch and strangles me with a belt.

Why am I so sad, snappy, irritable? Why won't this end, I just want to be happy.

End Script.

TMS Session 26

In my first session I try to think of some farm stories to give me a chuckle and wonderment on how we got through some of it.

There have been a few terrible snow storm April 30ths. I don't know why, but if there is going to be an epic snow storm, it is going to be on the day all of the tax accountants are finishing their work and starting to party. It also always falls around the time our first baby calves are born. One of the April 30ths I had gone out the night before to the tax party at the accounting firm I worked at. I barely made it home! It was snowing so hard you couldn't see the yellow lines on the highways. The girls were probably around the ages of four and six, and were tucked away in their beds when I got home at 2:00 in the morning. My husband Kevin was sleeping as well.

Very early in the morning (for a day off) I can hear Kevin yelling from the porch, "Everybody up! We need to get dressed and get outside."

If it had been April first and not May first I would have thought he was completely joking for April Fools day. I was so mad and I ran down the hallway saying, "Shhhhh, shhhh! Don't wake the girls!"

In a very serious tone, he said, "It doesn't matter. Everybody needs to get up get on their winter gear and get outside."

I quickly looked around and noticed the windows were all full of snow. You couldn't even see outside, and that the power was off. Kevin had already been outside, and said that about seven baby calves had been born in the snowstorm, and their mothers – through no fault of their own-- – had dropped them in the snow. As he walked past them checking them out, he saw that most of them were dead.

He told me to get in our big versatile tractor with a load of bales and to get out to the cows to start giving them bedding. Any other calves that we could find to save we should bring into the house. There have been a few times in my life that I felt like I was on *Little House on the Prairie,* and this was definitely one of them.

I put the girls in their little snowsuits and took them out with me in the tractor. I tried to follow Kevin's tractor's lead, but I couldn't even see two feet in front of me. I had never seen the snow blow so hard that it was a complete white out. I knew at one point that I was getting close to a gate, so I got out. I started walking, thinking I just had to make it to the gate. I was in snow up to my waist, while the wind and snow pushed against me. It felt like the wildest forces of nature pushing me back, but I plowed forward with my heavy Sorel boots and snowsuit. I made it to the gate and opened it, then got back in the tractor.

There I saw the girls cuddled in a little corner of the tractor. I knew we were going to be out there all day, and had no idea what they were going to do. It didn't take long though and they showed me their sense of adventure. The oldest, Kierra, pulled a hammer from the tool box and said something like, "Hi, Bob!" Then she grabbed a screwdriver in the other hand and introduced Kate the screwdriver to Bob the hammer. It wasn't long until the little one, Ava, joined in. Both girls had all the tools named and they played with them like they would play with their Barbies. I just had to giggle. In the worst snowstorm, with calves dying and their mother trudging through snow up to her waist, they had the resilience to know that they needed to think of something to do.

Throughout that day, sometimes I didn't even know if I was behind the house, to the north or south, but I trudged on and so did the girls. That night we had to wash and dry blankets repeatedly, and thankfully the power was back on. Kevin would bring us a calf so full of snow you could barely see their eyes, and we would run up and down the stairs with warm blankets from the dryer to warm them. The girls loved being by them. We fed bottles and kept them warm and safe through the night while Kierra slept under the table with them. In the morning, there was quite a lot of cleaning to do, as one calf had stood on his own, and had poop running down his back. It proceeded to walk through the kitchen, wiping the poop along the wall as it did. It was time for our houseguests to get the heck back outside after that!

In another April 30th snowstorm, Kevin was bringing baby calves to the house for us to warm up, but then wanted to take them back out to their mothers. He had a sled behind the snowmobile and I would hold the ninety pound calf in my lap tight and he would snowmobile out to the field. The funny part was that the snow would blow so much that it covered me and the calf both to the eyeballs, and every time we hit a bump, and the calf and I would jerk up in the sled and more snow would come in. I felt again like I was living on *Little House on the Prairie*, if they had a snowmobile back then! It was so ridiculous! When Kevin stopped the snowmobile, we were so fully covered with snow all you could see of me and the calf were our eyes! Kevin started laughing, and I couldn't do anything but laugh as well!

Sometimes some of the very worst times end with laughter.

****

In the second session after I read my script, I evaluate where I am.

I've had a good week for the most part. My mood is coming back up and my violent thoughts are fewer and a lot more under my control. I find now I can just say a quick "No" to myself when I envision a knife, rope or cord and it doesn't lead to any bad thoughts. Sometimes I have to say *no* a few times, but honestly, I'm getting a lot of my power back.

Another positive is that my moods no longer dip for long periods of time, or go way down. I am still up and down, but it's more of a bump on a graph instead of a mountain and a valley. Those valleys are so low…I hope I never have to see one again. I know I will though. This is a life-long struggle, and with stressors that just can't be avoided in life and all the uncertainties that exist, it will be a place I will probably re-visit again. However, I hope this time I learn the tools that get me out of there the fastest.

I can understand when you are that low that it feels like there is no hope. I've been there. I wonder if you could just for a minute in your lowest of lows imagine saying to a friend, "You can get better if you get help." But instead of talking to a friend, you are saying it to yourself. Day by day, hour by hour, imagine the medicine and treatment building that pathway in your brain to the logical side. Remember a time when you felt happy, and imagine if you could be there again. Imagine that the grass really is greener on the other side, because you created a path for that sad cow to get there. Sorry I couldn't resist the cow reference with the grass is greener. Lol. My bad.

  My brain feels like it is just full of pictures and thoughts. I can see maps. I spell letters by seeing them on a chalkboard in my thoughts. I also can see my brain, and I can envision those new pathways. I see the terrible and sad thoughts all stuck in one spot and I imagine them being pushed over to that logical side. You know you have the logical side because you know that in your history, you drew from that logical side for every exam you took, every presentation you made, every conversation you had. It's there. You must believe in it and in your own power to make changes.

TMS Session 27

Today in my session I start thinking how I find human bodies absolutely amazing. The more I learn about them, the more I am completely perplexed. Even when you are annoyed with your body because you are sick and shitting your pants, it is doing what it is supposed to be. It has to cause diarrhea in order to rid you of something harmful. In the case of me and my ischemic colitis, it cleans house so it can free the blood vessels where the blood flow is stuck. It first drains the blood in my face to look pale and yellowish, then takes more of the blood down to my colon to help fight. Isn't that cool? When you have the flu, your body has a fever and aches and makes you sleep for days because it is your immune response to the bug that is in you. It knows you need to rest, so it makes it impossible for you to move. You lay there quietly while it does its bug-fighting business.

I know mental health and physical health are connected and I know your body is doing everything possible to help you recognize you need help. Having stomach issues and chronic pain happens because your brain needs a rest and a re-set. Its pathways have been blocked by stress or cortisol and it is crying out for some help by sending messages to other parts of the body. It's saying to itself, "Shit your pants, then maybe she'll notice! Maybe she will get help, and maybe, just maybe, she will rest and work on her brain health."

This morning I looked out the window at our dog who goes insanely crazy every time I go for a walk. She is a farm dog so it doesn't really make sense because she could walk down our mile lane really anytime she wanted, but she waits for me to go. Then she gets so crazy that she is like a popcorn machine.

As I looked at her this morning, I thought, "What if I think that she is doing that because she wants to go for a walk, but she is really thinking, 'I better get mom out of the house and walking. She's been sad lately and she really needs my help. When she is outside with me, she smiles when the sunlight hits her face. I want to give her more of that.'"

Your brain and body are likely doing the exact same thing, but sometimes we aren't listening. I'm just slowly starting to listen again and let me tell you, for every moment my brain is at peace, I am so grateful. I imagine dancing now. I imagine being at a concert and throwing my hair around, laughing and smiling. And even if I'm still in the middle of the journey, and it's only for a few minutes, I'll take it. It's better than yesterday and the day before and the day before that. It's certainly better than it was in the middle of January, when I was in the emergency room. At that time I couldn't have even imagined writing this, as my brain was sending me such strong signals that it wanted to give in to the OCD compulsions and die. There is always, always hope. Five minutes today of pure bliss dancing around in my head, tomorrow I might get five more, the next day five more and in a few months, I'll be rocking at the concert and dancing like nobody's watching because I will be free.

****

I know stress exacerbates my OCD and depression symptoms. But the one thing I can't figure out is how to get rid of stress. Why do things make me stressed, and I don't even know that they do until they show up in my nightmares and symptoms? Why do I make choices that I know will cause stress? Am I afraid to live in a bubble, in a padded room, does it make me afraid to admit that I can't do as much anymore? We all do things that would be put in the category of being your own worst enemy. How do we stop making those choices?

I know some of my choices are about others having fun. It's not just the others though. I myself find events fun as well. They take prep and cleaning, making sure everything you need is bought, everything you are going to use is clean and ready to go. The weather can sometimes play havoc with your plans. It causes great stress making sure you have everything and everything will run smoothly and perfectly.

When you all have a great time, it is so blissful in those moments. You share a piece of yourself with everyone who has come to visit. You share the things that you love, and they get to enjoy it with you. Lots of times you want to share the nice things you have. Why be alone all the time to experience those magical things that you could share?

In the days following though, you are exhausted, snappy, irritable, cranky, and you struggle to find some peace again. The stress has done something to your body that others may not experience. It has made your brain suffer and you can't figure out why, because you were only sharing and doing what you enjoyed with people that you love.

What would happen if you were incapacitated by physical disability, and you could never share those things again? Would you ache for the things you used to do? I think of course you would. However, at some point you would have to accept your new reality, or the devastation of the loss would crush you. So, you forgo doing things that you love to do and you accept that life is the way it is and you simply can no longer take part in all the fun things that reflect the fun parts of yourself.

I don't believe it has to be an all or nothing approach for me, I guess simply because I don't want to give up. Do I have an impairment? Yes, I do. Do I need to accept that? Yes, I do. I don't want to give up though. I don't want to lie on the bathroom floor while my family enjoys the world around me. I've been there with my physical illnesses and I sure as hell don't want to do it again.

How do I make the choices that honor the stress I can actually handle? One thing you have to do is let others in, and I think you have to be vulnerable to your own reality. You have to admit that you can't do it all like you used to. I think you also have to reduce the expectations. Way easier said than done, in my head.

What if the people you loved and wanted to share things with saw all the parts of you? What if they saw the cobweb in the corner of the bathroom? What if they saw all your outdoor furniture covered in mud and hair from your shedding dog running in the muck and then jumping on the furniture? What if the entrances were full of mud because your little boy loves mud and drops his muddy splash pants and boots at a different door each time? What if the plates weren't really that clean because the dishwasher hadn't been working well and you keep trying everything you can to fix it? What if there were crumbs on the floor, in the cracks, under the table? What if there was dust on the TV stand? What if the plant was half dead and dropping leaves because you always forget to water it? What if there were dishes in the sink?

What if they might know that you struggle to do it all? What if they know that you want to have fun and share things with them, but it might not be clean or perfect? That at the last minute the sun will come out and it will be really warm, and you want to sit on the chairs outside that are full of spider webs, leaves and bird shit. What if then you asked them to help you clean those chairs and got them a pail with warm water and a rag? Would you do that for someone who was struggling to keep it all together but still wanted to have fun with you? Without a doubt, of course you would.

Why is it hard to ask for help and hard to look not perfect? Maybe stress is more about the mindset than the actual tasks at hand. I have been struggling trying to get our year-long invoices added up for tax, and the reality of it is that I've stressed and stressed and stressed about where I will come up with the time to do it. I have a month. Kevin thinks I'm being ridiculous, and I am. I told him the other day that the worst case scenario was that I work through the night of April 30 and put in eight or nine hours then to finish. Absolute worst case scenario. How embarrassing is it that I will stress myself out for a month over a task that literally could be done in an evening and night if I had no other choice. Then I will have to berate myself and my procrastination. Then I will put myself down repeatedly in all those hours thinking how stupid I was to wait so long.

That scenario has absolutely nothing to do with the task, and everything to do with my approach to it. Most of the overwhelm I feel in my life could be eased by changing the way that I think. How do you change the way you think, though, when you are so stubborn and so headstrong that things have to be a certain way? You have to lower your expectations, and how do you do that? You have to give yourself the grace that you deserve. The grace you would give others. Again, and a theme throughout this recovery period, loving yourself enough to lower your expectations and accept your mistakes is a key in changing your behavior.

If you choose self-care activities over your tasks that you need or want to complete, you need to accept that choice. You need to accept what it looks like to be a human full of faults. Let others see you with the cobwebs you are covered in. Let yourself see it. Then let others help you take some of the cobwebs off or just sit with you, covered in cobwebs. They are part of your outfit, whether you like them or not. You will never fully shed yourself of them. And if you ignore them, they will keep growing until they start to suffocate you. But if you leave the cobwebs, and brush them away slowly, or ask for help, they will stay manageable.

Stress is the root of my cobwebs, and I shall no longer let it grow over me and cover my eyes and choke me. I will practice living with it on me and letting others and myself see it. The spider needs some of the cobwebs to live and so do I.

TMS Session 28

There is a popular term to describe being jealous of where other people are and you aren't called "fear of missing out," or FOMO. I have always felt a sense of this, especially in the last 20 years. Is it social media that does this to us? Does it make us think that everyone is having a better time than we are? Why does it always look easier from the outside looking in?

It's like we are never peaceful with what we have – there is always the next thing. What is it about our society that we cannot just sit in stillness? Why do we always have to have something to look forward to? Summer? When the days are longer? A trip? Do we hate our lives so much that we can't be appreciative in our quiet moments and happy for others in their amazing moments? Amazing moments only last a short fraction of time and then everyone is back at work, looking after kids, cleaning and doing the daily grind.

If you were ninety looking back on your life, would only the amazing moments stand out and the rest be seen as useless time? Are you grateful for all the things or just the amazing ones? If you were standing in line when they were handing out roles for our souls and they said you could have ninety years of mediocrity, but with good friends and love, or you could have twenty years of an amazing life, with trips around the world, friends, riches, love, which would you choose?

If you couldn't hear, then the sound of the birds outside would be amazing. If you couldn't see, your friend's smile would be amazing. If you couldn't feel, a tight bear hug would be amazing. If you couldn't walk, your first steps would be amazing. If you couldn't talk, telling a story would be amazing. If you had only moments left to live, every single thing that was life would be amazing. I know it is a popular song by Tim McGraw, but what if we really lived like we were dying? Would you want your last moments to be seeing the Egyptian pyramids or saying good morning and hugging your child? Seeing the pyramids would be an amazing moment, but I wouldn't want it to be my last moment. If I accept that as true, then why would I ever have a fear of missing out?

****

When you have depression, it makes you feel doubly guilty when you can't enjoy things, big and small. It feels like you are taking it all for granted, but you can't stop. When you go through really low times, it's okay to be green with jealousy for the family that is in Hawaii or Mexico during their winter break. You hate yourself for feeling like that. It all comes back to self-hate and not giving yourself the grace and acceptance you need. When you are consumed with hate you can't see any good anywhere, in anything. It's not your fault though, so stop making it your fault. I'm literally just talking to myself and trying to make it stick in my head.

It's not your fault, let it go. The world is becoming clearer with every day. It won't be long, and you will get to a day where your brain will allow you to be 90% grateful for all the things, little or amazing. I say 90% because I don't want to shoot for 100% and then not meet my own expectations, Sometimes everyone has the nasties, guilt, shame, jealousy, and anger. It is human to have this full range of emotions. I believe the trick is to continue doing all that you can for the good emotions, the love, happiness, laughter, optimism, and let the nasty emotions have their place. Don't let the guilt of having them overcome you.

Think of it like this. Imagine you want to go for a walk but there is a terrible windchill outside. If you go out anyway, the cold will lash at your raw skin. It will burn, it will blind, it will feel unbearable. If you continue walking like that, your face will get frostbite and you will feel so guilty and shameful later. The wise thing to do is to turn around and go back and get a scarf. That way you can completely envelop yourself in the scarf and protect your face, skin and eyes.

It's the same thing if you go out every day and allow hatred, hopelessness, jealousy, and anger to hit you in the face. It will give you an emotional frostbite that will perpetuate your feelings of guilt, shame and hate. You will always be walking against the cold wind, and every step will hurt you more and more. By the end of your walk, your face will be unrecognizable because you chose to let it burn from the windchill.

I realize sometimes you can't see any other way but to keep walking like you always have. But you forgot about your scarf – self-help is your scarf. You may not find the right scarf immediately – some may be too short, too scratchy, the wrong color, but if you keep looking, you will find the right fit. With the right medicine, the right therapy, the right book, the right glimmer of hope, you can get a scarf that will keep you warm and toasty while you walk, and you actually enjoy it! And if one day it gets even colder, you will know where to find the hooded jacket and the face mask, and combined with the scarf, you will stay warm. Just believe for five minutes that your face is worth saving, and you will be able to also save your heart and your soul.

This is all coming from someone who just over a month ago felt so hopeless that her violent thoughts would never end that she didn't even feel the walk was worth it. But then she started looking for a scarf. First, she phoned a friend and admitted that she needed help. Then she put on some mitts by listening to doctors who had studied her condition. She tried some medication but it was like putting on ear muffs that didn't fit right, so she went and got a toque by starting TMS therapy. She got a warmer jacket by starting to journal out her feelings of life with illnesses. She put on warm boots by starting a gratitude journal so that every day that she felt worthless, had one little thing that she was grateful for.

Finally, she asked others to care for things so that she could start walking. Even though it was really hard to let go and not feel guilt and shame, she started her walk and the heaviness behind her eyes started to disappear. She could see the road more clearly than before and as she walked, her body became grateful. Every joint, every bone, every organ knew that she was helping them live, and she knew that one day soon she would be smiling. She was better off going on that walk no matter how hard it looked, because if she didn't, she would never know how good it felt when she got there.

Don't get me wrong. I know I still have a lot of walking to do, and I know that my face has been burnt over and over again by my depression and self-hate. I know I may need more than other people who walk on the same road at the same temperature. I might need heavier scarves, I might even need a full Helly Hansen -40 snowsuit! That's the part that is hard to accept. I don't want to need more protection than anybody else doing the exact same thing. But I don't get a choice, just like no one with any health challenges gets a choice. The best we can do is accept that even though we may be different, we can still live very successful lives in between the storms.

TMS Session 29

I imagine someone asking me, "Would you go to the lake if there was a chance of a storm? What if you knew for sure a storm was coming and there was nothing you could do to stop it? Would you go and enjoy the lake up until the point of the storm, or would you just stay home and not go to the lake at all?"

The answer is that I would definitely go to the lake. The storm would happen whether I was there or in my bed at home. I'd rather see the lightning glaring off the stormy water as I run in the rain to the car than to not have seen the lake, felt the sand on my heels and the warmth of the sun on my face. I'd rather have heard the sound of giggles from children, tasted the ice cream cone, and smelled the coconut sunscreen than not had the chance to swim in the water at all.

****

After my ischemic colitis attacks started happening a few years back, I realized there was a close connection between the attacks and alcohol. Dehydration is one of the factors, but given that you are supposed to drink 11 glasses of water a day, you are already at a deficit if you have coffee and alcohol, which interfere with your hydration. So I would have to have about 18 glasses of water to make up for it. So for the most part I just decided to stay away from alcohol.

But then when it had been almost a year since my last ischemic colitis attack, I started to have one or two alcoholic drinks again, and just tried to pound back the water to even things up. When everyone was drinking at Christmas, I was able to have a couple of beverages, which made me feel more like part of the gang! But then last January I had what I would call a breakdown. My OCD and violent imaging was out of control and suicide was becoming a lot more of a real idea and not just an image. Once I started TMS therapy, I went at least eight weeks with no alcohol at all. Since I had done it before, it didn't seem like a big deal, and really it isn't, except for certain occasions.

Alcohol makes me feel fun, free, rebellious, and silly. So much of my identity seemed to revolve around alcohol. When I was younger, I was the crazy one, the loud one, doing all my best tricks and jokes to get everyone laughing. Without alcohol I feel stale at a party, like the last crouton in the bag and the Ziploc hasn't been sealed. I don't feel like me. How is it that a mood-altering substance, which is supposed to be actually a depressant, makes me feel like me…the fun me, the happy me, the wild me. This me is so much more boring. I can't remember ever describing a night out without alcohol as "an absolute blast", or "crazy amazing." Even though when I don't have anything to drink I do wake up the next morning feeling good, I ache for the wild me, the free me, the silly me.

Maybe that is just a part of getting older. But I find that Kevin sure likes to drink like he did when he was younger. Last night we had over some of my daughter's friends that were all around twenty years old. Kevin partied with them in the hot tub until 3:30 a.m. I had a couple of virgin drinks and went to bed at 11:00 p.m. It was an okay night, but it just doesn't feel right not to join in with everyone.

TMS Session 30

I'm still thinking in my first session about the young, wild me and some of the fun, crazy stories about that time of my life. Of course, like most rural kids in the 1990s, we liked to party. However, I quickly realized what alcohol could do in the wrong amounts. I remember once my friends and I were planning to go to a party. My dad had some home brew stored in old containers downstairs behind the furnace. I took some and filled my empty and washed-out Clearasil and hairspray bottles with it. My friends and I started drinking and headed for the party. However, since we hadn't been invited to that party and we were younger than the hosts, we were immediately escorted out. I continued to pound my hairspray bottle back and snuck my way back in. By this time the home brew was hitting me hard, and when I got caught this time, the host grabbed me by the ear and threw me on the front step. I had alcohol rage for the first and maybe the only time I can remember. I started pulling out all the small trees, flowers and shrubs from the front yard, my hands full of cuts and scratches. Thankfully for me someone else on the lawn who had been kicked out stopped me from throwing a beer bottle into the picture window. I had taken aim and as it was coming out of my hands, they grabbed me by the elbow and told me to run because the cops were coming.

Another time, we were at a bush party out in a field on a farm. We had asked someone to pull us some beer from a nearby town. They took forever to get back to the party, so by the time the beer arrived, we only had about a half hour to drink six beers each. We were trying to drink it so fast that we were literally choking. Beer foam was coming out all of our noses while we sputtered and choked. I don't think we even ended up getting enough in our systems to feel a buzz before we left. When I look back on it I realize how dangerous it was, and how young and naïve we were!

Even when we were in university there were some times that I will never forget how dumb we were. My friends and I lived in an apartment about a half-mile from the bar. We used to walk there together, and often I would get drunk and decide I didn't want to wait for the other girls to go home. When I was ready to leave, I was ready! Many times I would start walking home alone. Once as I was heading to my apartment, I was so drunk that I fell in the snow. I lay there for probably ten minutes, then realized I was getting cold and got up and stumbled the rest of the way home. Another time when I was going home drunk, I went into the backyard of the wrong townhouse and entered some guys' party. There were like 20 guys there I didn't know, and I was like, "Oooops, wrong house!" They yelled at me to stay, but thankfully I didn't. Instead, I jumped the fence to our townhouse and was back in the safety of my locked door within minutes. If my daughters did stuff like that now, I would lose my mind.

One of my most famous stories from this time is when we were in second year university, and the Grey Cup Festival was being held in Regina. During the festival they have dances out by the stadium, and even though I had given blood that day, I still thought it would be a good idea to drink my face off before going. We didn't have tickets to the dances, so we used markers to color different plastic bands to wear on our wrists in order to fake our way in.

I ended up getting really drunk and somehow got separated from the rest of the girls. I bummed a cigarette off someone and was standing by myself in a corner smoking it when this cop came up to me.

He stared at me for a minute and then said, "You look like trouble."

For some reason I had to mess with him, and said, "You have no idea. I'm sixteen, I'm drunk and I snuck in here."

"Show me your ID," he responded.

But instead I started running. He chased me through the crowds of people and I ran into the women's bathroom. It connected to another dance in the other building, so I got through there and got away from him.

The funny part was I did have ID on me, and I was twenty and legal! I have no idea why I would make that up.

Later that night I finally found one of my friends. She was puking in a garbage can. I grabbed her and we headed out to some buses parked in the parking lot and climbed on board one of them. It was totally full except for two seats. We hadn't even looked to see where the bus was going, but just sat down and immediately fell asleep. Later we were awoken by the bus driver who said he was at the last stop. We looked around and there was no one left on the bus but us. We had no idea what city we were in, but we got out. I threw up behind the bus while my friend looked around at our surroundings. We found that we were just a few miles from home, so we decided to hitchhike. I would never, ever do that now, and if my kids did I would lose it. But somehow we made it home alive.

Another time a friend and I had the crazy idea to go to the liquor store in our pajamas. We bought some champagne, and we were going to continue to party, but for some unknown reason as we were driving back, we decided to take off our bras and throw them out the window of the car. After we did, we realized how dumb it was, and whipped a U-turn to go back and get them. When we got there, we saw that they had been driven over like five times, so we thought it was best to just go home and forget about it.

****

I know these stories seem dangerous and stupid now, but it felt so free! Is there a way to still feel that free? Is there a way to forget who you are for just a little bit? Sometimes I really understand how people become addicted to alcohol and drugs, because the feeling of being free is so desirable. The problem is, of course, that it doesn't just last one night. It is dangerous, physically and mentally.

So how do I find her again? How do I find that silly, happy, wild girl without resorting to drinking or taking drugs? Is she gone forever? Am I just old now, and all that is in the past, just crazy wild memories? I have to find her again. She must still be here somewhere.

TMS Session 31

Probably part of finding that girl I used to be has to do with liking the person I actually am now. I think I made a breakthrough the other day. Kevin was telling a friend how tough it is living with someone with depression, and how sometimes my not being aware of things is hard for him. I thought whatever he was going to say was going to make me upset. I was all ready to feel criticized, which would lead to me being self-critical. But I was surprised to find that it didn't! Kevin explained to his friend how he gets really frustrated when I don't notice a mess, and therefore I don't clean it up. He said that for days I had walked by some yoghurt containers that he had used to feed the cats. I almost walked over them when I went outside, but I never picked them up. I don't even remember this happening, but my breakthrough is that I really could not care less! That is something new for me, and I'll take it!

I actually think it's funny that in my darkest hours, after being sick for several years while handling work, kids, and all of life's responsibilities, that the worst thing I did was walk past yoghurt containers and not pick them up! Honestly, if that is the worst thing you have to say to me after all of this, holy crap am I happy. Now a few months ago I would have become defensive. I would have given you 100 reasons why I was so busy that I couldn't pick up the containers. But today I just want to shout out, "Whoooo hoooo! I'm such a terrible loser that I didn't pick up the yoghurt containers!"

****

During the second part of my session, when I went from my positive thoughts to my negative script, I noticed my innate defensiveness rearing its ugly head. It seems like any time I have small victories, they are met with an underlying current of emotions that lash out at me. It's like something doesn't want me to have small victories because it means I am winning. Why must this fight be so difficult?. I was feeling pretty good that the worst thing I had done recently was walking past old yoghurt containers on the ground and not picking them up. But then I felt like fighting back for some reason. I found myself wanting to lash out at him. Last night I noticed some Cheetos that he had dropped on the floor by the couch, and I wanted to take a picture of them and send it to him and say, "Are you ever going to clean this up or are you waiting for your mommy to do it?"

I guess when Kevin questions any of my actions or decisions, my guard automatically goes up. I want to say, "How dare you question me?" as if it signals judgement towards me instead of just being a difference in opinion. Can we just have differences without one being right and the other one feeling she is so wrong and stupid that she wants to crawl into bed for eternity?

It really goes back to me feeling like I have to defend myself for every action or opinion. Like somehow, I don't trust myself, so I get defensive to prove that I am right. What would happen if I had an open mind, and if we could have conversations instead of me feeling judged and then fighting to win?

When can I just like myself enough so that I can also be wrong? When can I be wrong without telling myself I am stupid? And when will I realize that sometimes nobody is wrong, and it literally is just a difference of opinion?

I need to realize that I have flaws, and I am still worthy of love. I need to love myself, mistakes and all. For the record, Kevin is not wrong. I do walk past and ignore lots of things. I do ignore a fridge full of rotting food and just keep shutting the door. I always feel there are so many chores that I could do on any given day. If it's not the fridge today, it will be another day. Tomorrow comes and it isn't the fridge that day either, it's something else. Then when someone mentions that the fridge is dirty, I blow my top and tell them all the things I have been doing around here, and ask them why no one appreciates all the things I have done. And I'm mad. I'm mad because I didn't actually clean the fucking fridge when I noticed it was dirty. I'm mad about the dirt on the wall I just walked by. I'm mad about the clothes lying in my room that need to be put away or cleaned. I'm mad at the toys all over the floor. I'm mad about the spilled popcorn in Brant's room that I know is there but I walk by it.

I'm mad because someone pointed out a flaw that, according to Kevin, goes back to my childhood and my parents, to my being spoiled and thinking that someone is actually coming to clean up my mess, but they never show up. He thinks I need someone to pick up my mess because I am incapable of doing it myself. I'm useless, I'm lazy, I'm a loser, I'm spoiled rotten, I have zero work ethic, and I love to live in pig pens.

It stuns me that a yoghurt container left on the ground can lead to such trauma after 30 years of being together. I feel like no matter what I do, I'm wrong. If I walk past it, I'm a lazy, self-centered human, incapable of looking after my responsibilities. If I pick it up, I'm annoyed, and resent the fact that I didn't put the container there, and ask why is everything all of a sudden my duty to clean up? How about if I pick up my own shit and you pick up your own shit, and then we can both be responsible adults in our home, with nothing to give rise to judgement of the other person?

Here's another example of why I feel judged. Last week I cleaned the bathroom, organized the shelves, cleaned underneath them, and did the same for the medicine chest. Then I stood on the counter to wipe down the inch-thick dust off the top of the mirror and the light fixture. After that I came down to make everyone lunch. For some reason I wanted accolades for the work I had done, and possibly a parade in my honor for cleaning the light fixture. Instead, I was met with, "There is still fly poop all over it! You need to scrub it, not just wipe over it!"

"Fuck you," I think. "I did all of this for an hour and that is what you have to say?"

Any possibility of external validation got literally kicked into the toilet. I could see it floating there. But where is my internal validation? All I can think is, "Okay so not only is the trophy and the parade not happening, I didn't even clean the light fixture well enough. Now I'll have to do it again!" What I should be thinking is, "That was the best that I could do with the time I had, so fuck external validation!"

I have to think of an analogy to make this stick. Let's say I love Juicy Fruit gum, and I buy it for myself and I chew the sweetness out of it and then throw it away because I'm done with it. Should it bother me if you think that I didn't chew the gum long enough? I chewed it long enough for me, I got what I wanted out of it. I know if you had been chewing it, you would have chewed it until your jaw was raw to make sure you got the most out of it. But I'm fine with how long I chewed mine. Do we have to berate or judge each other for being different? Can I still love my chewing experience and not feel I did something wrong by doing it differently?

Do we have to blame childhood experiences? "Oh you never know the worth of things! Do you think your Mommy and Daddy are always going to buy you new gum when you don't chew the one you have until your tooth aches?"

Or what if, even worse, I put TWO sticks of gum in my mouth! "Okay, now you are crazy. You're over the top! What's wrong with you? How wasteful!"

"But I like two pieces! It doubles the sweetness, and it makes me smile as I chew it."

Can we each agree that we chew gum differently and no one is right, and no one is wrong? Can I still have the self-worth to know that I can enjoy something because that is the way I do it and not all people do it the same way?

While we were fighting about the chewing gum in my analogy, an earthquake happened in Japan, people froze to death on a highway when their car broke down, a baby was born to someone who thought she was infertile…life goes on. Every snowflake is unique, and if we all chewed gum the same way, the world would be all the same. If there were no personality differences and no past experiences that were different, we would be walking, talking, gum-chewing robots and I'm pretty sure we were each given our uniqueness for a reason. My uniqueness doesn't have to be better or worse than yours; it is just mine.

TMS Session 32

If you Google *how do you get self-love?*, be ready for a new super-long checklist! All I can think is, "You mean I have to do all this in addition to drinking water, brushing my teeth, exercising, taking my meds, going to therapy and the hundreds of other things already on my to-do list? Where do I start?"

Well, I have talked about a few so far, like forgiving yourself for your illness. I also have been journalling, so that's two. You are going to say, "What about your gratitude journal? You're doing that, right?" Well I have fallen behind on it. That figures, right? Maybe if I had just kept up with it, I would love myself wholeheartedly by now. Hahaha.

******

I keep thinking of the self-love list and it looks like a mountain to me.

When we toured Australia in my mid-twenties, we went to a place in Alice Springs called Ayers Rock. In the early 2000s, you could actually hike up, but now I am told it is sacred and no one can climb it anymore. The day we were there, all I had packed was sandals. We arrived at sunrise and had planned a magical experience of hiking to the top. As we started climbing straight up this steep rock, I began to slip. Then I slipped again. I turned around to see how high we were and saw that we had barely made any progress up the rock. I was scared, and told Kevin I wouldn't be able to do it. I kept slipping, and the height scared me. I ended up sliding back down on my bum, and Kevin went on to the top without me. I sat there thinking about what the sunrise must look like from the top. I often think about that day, and wonder if I had ever gone back there again if I would have sucked it up and climbed the rock. It's something most people in the world can only dream about doing. In all likelihood though, I probably would have started out again, freaked myself out again, and still ended up sliding down to the bottom on my bum.

I want to start the self-love journey, but as you can see from my writing, I always keep slipping back. Should I ride my bum down and just forget it? Should I force myself to try to get to the top and see how magical it could be? What awaits me at the top? What if that really fun-loving girl I once was is up there? Could I find her again?

What if I worked really hard at that list, and went step by step. Every time I slipped backwards I would then step forward again, and again, until finally I was able to find glimpses of her. Would that be enough to make me keep going? As my TMS treatments continue, sometimes I catch just a quick glance of her. Out of the corner of my eye, there she is smiling, sitting on the beach, listening to music, not a care in the world. Her hair is messy and tangled from the wind, her sunscreen not all the way rubbed in around her cheek, but she doesn't care. She doesn't care about anything, she is in love with the present moment. She is in love with the warmth of the sun on her skin. She smiles as she watches her husband and children play in the ocean. She has everything and her heart is truly full, and her brain is at peace. If I can see her for a few minutes, is it worth the climb? I think I would rather die trying than to never see her again. She is so beautiful, so loving, so loved. She is everything I ever wanted to be. She is me, but she is just temporarily trapped behind some brain pathways, and they are starting to open.

I can almost feel her. "Keep going," she says. "Keep going, I am here. I'm going to find you, my girl, and when I do, I will treat you better, I promise. I loved you first and I will love you until your dying breath. I was the one who first saw your mommy's eyes with you. I was the one who felt what it was like to sit on Daddy's lap. I saw the moon with you, I made dreams with you. I watched all the sunsets with you. You, my dear narrator, have never left. I used to hate your narration, you were so filled with hate. You never left me though, through the darkest times, through the hurt and pain, through all my slurs against you, you stayed. I will finish looking at my children's eyes with you, giving my husband a kiss with you, hugging my mom and dad with you, smiling at my friends with you, until the end. It's you and me and I wouldn't want it any other way. We are who we are not because of it, but in spite of it. We are who we are. We see life through a different lens, and even blurry lenses can take some amazing pictures."

TMS Session 33

Einstein said the definition of insanity is doing the same thing over and over again and expecting different results. I start reading through some old journals I wrote, and I see the same things repeated throughout my life. The quote instantly comes to my mind. Isn't it insanity that I have never truly figured out how to like myself in all these years? I look at a few journals from 1989 to 2010 and the theme is always the same.

- I need to lose weight. I eat too much, I eat crap food, I keep making myself fatter, I look in the mirror and see someone who looks fatter every day – it's my biggest failure and always has been.

- I feel like I don't do anything right, everyone seems to want a piece of me, I'm exhausted being the good worker, smiley co-worker, keeping home life together, good daughter, good sibling, good in law.

- Being always happy and smiling is exhausting, especially when you want to lie down and cry.

- Having non-stop suicide thoughts. I don't want to die but I can't live with this self-hatred and pain.

- Feeling like my kids are sick more than others because I am not clean enough.

- Not being good at anything, constantly making mistakes.

- Feeling sad that my girls are going to grow up with a mother so mentally unstable.

- "This is 2010, the year to love me."

Well that last one makes me sick to my stomach. 2010 was the year to start loving myself and here I am in 2024 in the exact same spot. What can I do differently that I haven't tried before? How do I get out of Einstein's insanity loop? There has to be some difference this time around. I don't want another 14 years to go by and be in the exact same spot. In 2038, when I am 63, please let me not be reading this and thinking I am in the same spot. Please let me have learned from all of this. Please tell me the pathways that are starting to open in TMS stay open and I stay committed to my self-care.

****

I think of my autograph book I had when I was a child. My Aunt Elaine wrote a quote in there probably when I was around 10: *Your future lies before you like a path of driven snow, be careful how you tread it because every step will show.*

I have always pondered this quote. Does it mean you should be careful in the choices you make and where they will lead you? I imagine the path of snow behind me and my footprints on it, and feel like at this point in my life, all you would see were footprints going in circles. Girl, you are so lost. The quote didn't mean not to walk forward at all because you're scared of the choices. It meant that if you don't start going forward in the snow, the path that you look back on may lead nowhere. Thinking about it now, it finally makes sense to me – make the choices that take you in the right direction, don't make the choices that lead you back where you started.

What if I give this message to myself, and use it as a guiding light down the path: keep going forward and keep doing the things that are working. You are starting to make a few steps down the path. Keep going but this time don't stop! Don't stop walking, don't stop trying, don't stop believing that maybe this time you'll get to the cabin at the end of the path, the warm cabin that has blankets and a stoked-up fire, a cup of hot chocolate, and all your family and friends sitting on couches waiting for you to arrive.

TMS Session 34

Knowing how hard these treatments were when I first started and how I cried through the first ones makes me think about how bad ass I actually am. I realize that being stubborn is sometimes a good thing. I felt this very strongly last night as I danced around the kitchen to the old Belinda Carlisle songs "Heaven is a Place on Earth" and "We Got the Beat." I felt so good that I wanted to shout it from the rooftops, and wanted everyone to feel like I did. But my feeling good at that moment made me also realize that it's important to know that what is working for me might not work for everyone.

For example, I read something this morning about repeating self-affirmations every day, and even getting your children to say them. But while saying *I am strong, I am confident, I am courageous, I am brave* might work for some, it doesn't work for me. In fact, it pisses me off that some people believe you can think your way out of this disease. If I made affirmations every night that I would never get endometriosis, would I never get endometriosis? If I made affirmations that I would never die of a heart attack, would I never die of a heart attack?

The one thing no one tells you about self-affirmations is that the person saying them has to be receptive to them. They may not work for me because I'm not made like that. I know a month ago, when everyone was encouraging me and I was trying to encourage myself, it was like we were talking to cement. Talk to the wall, talk to the stairs, talk to the floor, talk to the couch, see if they believe the self-affirmations. I was the couch, made of cold leather, an exterior that won't soak in anything. Pour a Coke on a couch…what happens? It doesn't sink in, it just dribbles and rolls off onto the floor. How do you make the couch absorb the liquid? The only way the Coke will seep in is if you cut open the leather and expose the padding underneath.

My depression is the self-hating, self-loathing leather. I could tell myself a million times that I was strong and courageous, and do you know what my leather exterior will say? "No you are not. You are a worthless, lazy, spoiled, stupid, sack of shit."

I have gotten a little bit closer to believing the affirmations through breaking open the pathways in my brain. For the most part, the negative voices in my head that are caused by my depression were always louder than anything else. Even the logical side of my brain wasn't able to fight against these voices. It was like David and Goliath. I wonder how David got strong enough to fight Goliath?

For me, some things work and some don't. Some things might work today but not tomorrow. And it's different for everyone. What I do know is that between TMS, daily therapy, going off work, focusing on myself, daily writing, my gratitude journal, my OCD app that gives me exercises every day, the support of family, work, and friends, I can finally say that my logical voice is louder than the depression voice. But I didn't get here without putting everything I had into it.

****

You may be asking yourself how you can help a loved one or yourself. I don't have the answer for everyone. How do you make David want to fight Goliath in the first place? It would be easier for David to just hide under the covers. What if you told David that other people had beat Goliath? That would probably really help. And if David has faith in himself, he will already be halfway there. Faith in any form to any higher purpose will make some part of you believe that you can do it.

I am pondering that saying about how you can lead a horse to water, but you can't make him drink. The truth is you just can't make anyone drink, just like you can't make the Coke seep into the leather. But maybe if you didn't feel alone in your fight, maybe if just for one minute you could put faith in the fact that David did beat Goliath, you might see that what has been done can surely be done again. You are not the first and you are not alone. David had his higher power because he believed and had faith in it. What if you could be David, and even though you had tried everything else, you tried again. You took some medicine, and it was like a sword, but it was too small to cut into Goliath's legs. You tried some therapists, and they were like some rocks you threw at Goliath's feet. You tried TMS, you tried journalling, but you never tried them all at once. You had never tried new things like Ketamine therapy. Maybe one of those combinations is the slingshot that has the rock that will hit Goliath square between the eyes and give you back your power.

And remember that when you get back the power, it won't always be easy to keep it. But just getting back the power to fight against the terrible depression voices is so undeniably satisfying. It's like punching the bully you always wanted to punch, getting an A plus on the math test, getting to the top of a mountain on a hike, or laying in the sun listening to the ocean. It's a true feeling of pride in yourself that no self-affirmation can give you.

Cut open the couch and see what's inside. You can fix all the layers in it and then you can sew it back up. It might not be exactly the same couch, but you will have gotten to the root of the problem and seen how to fix it. Find the faith of David, knowing there is something higher than all of this physical brain stuff, and use that faith to fix the physical brain stuff so you can fight the giant.

I had signs along the way to keep going, and I truly believed them. In some of my darkest moments I would find a dime lying in front of me. For me, dimes and pennies are a signal from up above that you need to keep going. I could feel someone above me was saying I should stay the course and keep going. Once when I was at a very low point sitting on the floor in my storage room wanting to give up, I picked up some tissue paper and out fell a dime and two pennies. I fully believe these signs are a way for our souls to give us hints and clues that we are going in the right direction, and we just need to keep going.

I believe another sign came the other day from my in-laws, who have now passed away. I have many special cards that I have saved over the years in different boxes in storage. The other day when I was looking for an old journal of mine to read, a card popped out of a box and fell into my lap. It was from my mother- and father-in-law, from my graduation in 1993. They had only known me for about seven months when they sent it, and their words rang out like a bell in a chorus. Just seeing my mother-in-law's writing made me smile:

Michelle! (Yes, it had an exclamation mark!)
If you can just keep smiling
When the world can use a smile.
If you can give some meaning
To your efforts all the while.
If you can face each challenge
With the courage you possess.
If you can help somebody
Find the road to happiness.
If you can live your lifetime
With a spirit young and free
You'll be the special person
That you always hoped you'd be.

There it was, the affirmation that I was actually ready to hear. It didn't roll off the leather. Because of all the work I had already done cracking open the depression, it sank right in.

You'll be the special person that <u>you always hoped you'd be.</u>

Not what anyone else hoped I'd be, but what I hoped I'd be. All the things that I said I wanted – to be young and free again, a purpose to help others – it was handed to me like a message that fell from the sky.

TMS Session 35

It is scary that it had to get to such an insanely dark and terrible point before I got the help I needed. Last May we had some executives at work telling their mental health stories. I decided to share mine as well, but something about saying it out loud made me start to spiral down. That moment was like a catalyst of something starting to change in me. Then in January when I started writing out my story, I again spiraled completely down to my breaking point. What was it about admitting my struggle to myself and others out loud that pushed me over the edge? Somehow, when it all came pouring out of me, the logical side of my brain said, "Hey, what's going on over there?" Whatever it was, it started my own revolution.

While I don't think of myself as two people, I do feel like there are two parts of my brain: the one I call "the narrator" and the one I call my soul. The narrator is part of my physical brain, but my soul is unexplainable. It's not like a thought but like an energy field. My soul does not have the power to change the thoughts in my brain, but it is like a silent cheerleader, trying to give hints and signs to move in the right direction. I wanted to blame the narrator today for all the terrible images I was seeing, but it wouldn't accept it because the narrator has been there all along. The narrator is held hostage while the OCD and depression are throwing stones at it. It wanted to be free, but it didn't know how, and its enemies are too powerful.

As the narrator starts to take control again, it is using the more logical parts of my brain that have been hidden. With the poison I was feeding it, the narrator could only survive, not flourish. It had no idea that there even was a different pathway, it had been blocked for so long. That path was covered in trees and shrubs and rock, and looked like no one could ever get through it. But little by little, some of the rocks moved and some of the shrubs were uprooted. Then some of the trees were chainsawed, and the narrator saw that there was an actual pathway after all. The more the pathway opened, the more the brain wanted to take a chance to see what was there. I feel like it needed to be blown wide open before any progress could be made.

That's why I think this time I'm not going to go round and round on the path behind me. This time I will keep moving forward. Will there be stuff along the way that tries to close the pathway again? Yes, there will be stress boulders, and unexpected worries will start to grow the trees, but the difference this time is that the narrator knows they exist. So when a boulder pops up, it can look back on its history and say, "This thing needs to get hauled out of here! We need some more self-care to keep this path open." What can never happen again is for the path to close so tightly that it no longer exists. Since we have broken it open this time, we know it's there.

In the last year, I have learned how OCD and depression can go up and down for years. Many times things have been unbearable, but now that I have these new tools, I know I can find my way out. I have the support of my family that I never had before. I also have the support of many friends, people at work, and a professional support team. All of this has given me the power to get away from the beast that has plagued me. This time I know what the beast is, and I know how to defeat it. There will be no more going around in circles. There is only a path forward, with a few minor breaks along the way to kick some rocks. I also won't forget to bring my chainsaw.

****

When I hit my breaking point in January and started TMS therapy, the first thing I had to do was complete some surveys about my symptoms and their severity. I remember doing the same survey in May of the previous year when my psychiatrist first diagnosed me with OCD. One of the questions is: *How often do you control your obsessive thoughts: never, rarely, half the time, most of the time, all the time.* I thought to myself both times that I didn't understand the question. They ask the same question about compulsions, and again, since my compulsions are my thoughts, I didn't understand the question. What do you mean control your thoughts? They appear out of nowhere and they control me. How would I ever have any other answer besides never?

My OCD obsession thoughts are of someone, usually someone I love with all my heart, being hurt or killed. My OCD compulsion thought to go with it is to immediately stab or hurt myself in some way to make it stop. It doesn't stop though, and it goes round and round sometimes hundreds of times an hour. I had even asked my psychiatrist once what to do when the thoughts won't stop coming, and he simply said, "Say no." I thought at the time, "What an odd thing to say for a professional who knows these thoughts are uncontrollable."

In fact, until this very week I believed they were in control, but for the first time ever, I chose the answer *sometimes*. What? I can't believe it! You mean I really can control them? I thought back over the previous few weeks, and the number of times I had said *NO!* to the thought, and it left me alone. So yes! Sometimes I have control!

This week I feel even in more control. All I have to do is say, "No, I'm not going there," and it stops. It is profound to me that this is happening. I am elated!

You know when you are sick with the flu or throwing up, how every minute is like a torture. I know that with my endometriosis and bowel attacks, I have spent many nights praying for just one minute to pass, then two minutes, then three… Then the next day when you feel better, you are so grateful, but it doesn't take long to forget how painful it actually was. You forget how every minute was a minute where you felt like you just needed to make it one more minute.

But most of us don't walk around every day being grateful that today is not one of those sick days, that today our stomach has digested its food and our intestines are doing their job properly. The lungs, heart, and blood vessels are all doing a good job today. It's only when you are going through it that you are so grateful when it stops. I feel like that with my brain. Sometimes I almost forget how much hell it actually was, how I felt so low and so out of control that I believed I wasn't going to make it. Looking back now, it feels very sad, but I am so grateful.

When you are in it, you can't think of not being in it, and when you are out of it, you can't imagine being in it. That is why people drink again the next Saturday night even when they had a terrible hangover this weekend and swore they would never drink again. It is why we have another baby after kind of forgetting the whole process. Our brains and bodies are so resilient that when it's over, it feels like it was a lifetime ago. You think, "I'll give it a go again. I did it once, I can do it again."

My mood feels so elevated right now that I feel like if the OCD and depression hit me again, I could fight. However, when I was in the middle of it, I felt like I had no fight left in me. I was so exhausted that I thought I and everyone else would be better off if I wasn't here anymore. For the people who think about suicide, that is where their road stops and they are just done fighting it. Having been through it myself, I know that you don't think there is another day that you won't be in that much pain and torture. If you had control of your thoughts, you would tell them, "Get lost. I know a better tomorrow is coming. It always does. I've fought this before, and I can fight it again."

I feel like I just want to help people get to where I am now, with no heaviness behind my eyes, no violent thoughts, no torture. I'm part of an OCD group on Facebook, and many times someone will post that they are finished with life. When I see those posts, I want to shout out to them that there is hope! But I feel helpless. I don't actually know for sure what changed in my brain, and my combination of things may not be the same as theirs. I wish I had some kind of inspirational message or something magical that would snap people out of the control that their thoughts have over them. But there is no magical solution. I hope that by sharing my story, maybe, just maybe, one day someone might grab that wee bit of control that they have, and see that I did it and it's possible for them, too. It's not an easy road, but maybe for some, the hope that they could have control again would be enough to save them. I do believe my purpose after having fought these diseases is that I can help someone else get the strength to fight their own battles.

TMS Session 36

To date I have had 36 TMS visits, which equals 72 treatments. I began on January 17, and it is now March 14. The first few weeks were very hard, but I was told it would get better. It did! When I first started, my mood was from 3 to 5 out of 10, every day. Sometimes I cried all the way through the session from physical and emotional pain.

When I talk to my tech today, we discuss how far I have come, and she says that I am a different person today than when I walked in there. It's miraculous but I'm scared to jinx it.

I am so grateful that I am experiencing what a "normal" person's brain feels like. I say that because sometimes I still find it hard to believe that other people don't have thoughts of harm, self-hatred, constant guilt, anxiousness, restlessness, all the things that I experience.

Right now, it feels like a blank slate that I get to choose what to write on. I never even knew it was possible to feel so calm, relaxed, and joyful. I know it won't stay forever but just getting a full taste of it right now makes me so excited for the future.

As the first session starts today I decide to work out something that I read the other day. It said that children love their parents more than parents love their children. I don't know if that is true, but there is one thing I know for sure – we are always trying to get assurance out of our parents. Maybe that's not true for all, but a lot of people I know search and search for a way to get their parents to approve, accept, and love them as they are. As far as I am concerned, parents don't do that in return to their children. I don't know many people who constantly seek reassurance of their children's love, and if they don't get it, they begin to seek it from others, and end up having a poor self-image. This may be more true of children from my generation or older, whose parents were all more closed off, and didn't discuss feelings or emotions. We were essentially left on our own when it came to our thoughts and feelings. I'm not blaming my parents for this, but it was a generational theme.

Kevin and I were watching a show about Nazi Germany and World War II the other night, and I told him how scared I have always been of these shows. It hurts me to my core to think of people being that evil to other humans. It made me think back to when I was little and my family was watching *Sophie's Choice*. I was probably around eight years old at the time and some of the images in it never, ever left me. There were people getting shot, and being pulled from their hiding spots in their homes and put on trains to go to the death camps. The choice Sophie had to make was whether she wanted her daughter or her son to live, and if she didn't make the choice, they would kill them both. Who can even imagine how evil you would have to be to do that to someone. Anyway, after that movie I was always scared when I heard trains, thinking that at some point they were going to come and get us to take us to one of those camps. At that age I didn't really understand why that happened, and gosh, I guess I still don't. In my child's eyes I was scared it would happen again and this time they would come for us.

  I tell this story because I am 48 years old and have never told it to anyone. I never said that at night I used to look out my window to see if they were coming to get us. Again, I'm not blaming my parents, because this was our generation, but I never discussed the things that scared me. I never asked them if I should be scared that it would happen to us. I didn't tell my brothers and sister, kids at school or anyone else. I just grew up being afraid of that, along with many other things I didn't understand and couldn't process alone.

  With no one available for our emotions, we held them all in, ill-equipped to make sense of them. We essentially parented ourselves when it came to feelings and emotions. We loved our parents beyond measure and were always trying to be our best for them. We were constantly guessing at what that perfection looked like, because they never said. We knew when we did things wrong, but we didn't know when things were right, so we constantly strived to prove how good we were. It was never enough though, because we never knew what they thought of what we did. Maybe they were amazingly proud and thought we were smart, strong, and everything they hoped we would be, but they just never said it out loud. Like no one ever said, "I love you." You don't discuss your feelings with each other.

What was it about those generations that made it so wrong to speak about your emotions? What was so wrong with sharing your feelings? I'm guessing they were also raised that way. In fact, it was even more authoritarian for them. They certainly didn't have parents telling them how proud they were of them. When they were eight years old they were chopping firewood, feeding the chickens, doing all kinds of chores. They would have considered themselves lucky they hadn't been yelled at or kicked that day, and that they got to have a warm bed to sleep in. So, in fact it is no surprise that they believed they were giving us the world in our childhoods to be free to be kids. That is what my mom says that she always wanted for her children. There is no doubt our childhoods were better than theirs.

I do believe there is that balance between authoritarian and permissive parenting. It isn't good for children to grow up in one extreme or the other. When parents are too authoritarian and the child can never do anything right, they either end up rebelling or have all kinds of self-image issues. If they're too permissive, the child will never understand having rules or respecting authority, and will be left with a poor self-image, because even if they are told repeatedly how much they are loved, they don't feel that they have earned it for themselves.

****

When I had to start thinking of my script and negative things today, I thought back to my time as an articling student, working to gain experience in accounting. In my career when you started as a junior accountant, you were treated like a dog on a leash. The theory was that the dog will only behave for you if you tell it exactly what to do, rub its nose in its own shit, and kick it if it doesn't obey. Eventually the dog will learn the rules and be the perfect puppy. Ha! And eventually that dog is going to want to bite you in the ass as well! In accounting we always got notes on what we did wrong with each file, and sometimes we would get like twenty notes of what we did wrong. It was very humbling, to say the least.

You also had to dress to a certain standard, wearing women's suits and the proper footwear when out on the road. If you failed to follow this, you would be majorly barked at. You were constantly reprimanded for not saying something correctly to the business owner, for using the wrong color pen, for stamping something the wrong way, or for spelling something wrong. You had to love working from 8:00 a.m. to 1:00 a.m., coming home on a stormy winter night, then getting up at 6:00 a.m. the next day to do it all over again. Yes, it also taught us that by the time we received our Chartered Accountant certification we would be more than worthy. Then it would be our turn to be the teacher and kick the little dogs around. Except that I never wanted to kick little dogs. I wanted the little dogs to love their life. I always tried in my management style to remember what it felt like to be at the bottom and to have no one there with a kind voice and a willing hand to help me along.

In my management style, I want my staff to want to work for me. I want them to pitch in and work until 1:00 a.m. because we are a team. I want them to want to help me do the job because they respect and like me, not just because they are being paid to do it. There are rules, of course, and everyone needs to abide by those rules, and I should be a leader in respecting those rules. I believe that you can be a balance of both – strict and understanding. There should be no place for criticism that is not helpful, no belittling or making others feel dumb, no making yourself seem more important, or any negative behavior. Any shortcomings should be addressed and a plan put together to get the job done in a faster, more accurate or better way. Managers should always admit when they did wrong or when they could have helped avoid something that happened. They must work with the staff to sort out how they can do better going forward. Managers should help get the most potential out of their employees by being their biggest cheerleader, challenging them, pushing them along, and doing so with tact. I guarantee if you are this type of manager, your staff will do everything you want them to do and more. They will always have your back. If it doesn't turn out this way, then there is a good possibility that they are just in the wrong career and may have aspirations different from what you can provide.

As a parent I do the same thing for my children…except they don't get to choose to leave me for a new career choice! Haha. I want them to know and respect rules and be a helpful person in society and I want to be their biggest cheerleader. I want them to be challenged and proud of themselves. I want them to know that no matter what, my love is unconditional. Even when they fail, I will be there to help them get back up. After all, if we don't fail, we just aren't trying hard enough.

TMS Session 37

I know there is going to be a learning curve as I find a way out of this hole that I fell into. As I have tried many different ways to get to the top, often my foot has slipped and my hands have been left grasping at grass or twigs. Today was day 37 of my TMS treatment and unfortunately, it was another tough one. I have a few built-up anxieties that feel stronger than me. It's like they can see that one little push and I'll fall farther and farther down the hole. They look for my weak moments, the moments that I start to feel a bit off my game, and they start making their way back in. They want me to take hold of them and give them back the power. They are my opponents in this war, and I am garnering my strength to fight them.

They lashed at me last night with scary thoughts before bed. I saw Brant being choked, lying beside me in bed and turning blue. In the morning, they showed me a bunch of knives, and when I said *No!* they pointed out every single knife all around me as if to say, "Take that! You won't get away with your little *no* this time."

So when I arrived at TMS, I discussed with my tech how to stand up to these awful things that are trying to weasel their way back in. She said they will always try when you are vulnerable, and you need to fight back to show them they have no power.

It wasn't hard to get worked up to start the treatment today. My mind had again begun flashing violent images against me. At one point my wrists were bound and I was hanging from a barn-like structure, fully naked. A serial killer came in and started to torture me in the worst ways possible. He cut off pieces of my legs and arms and then cut both of my breasts off with a thick rusty old knife. The blood trickled all down my body and my breasts lay on the floor in a pile with my other skin and tissue. Then he decided to gut me like a pig and bind my feet and hang me upside down to bleed out until I died. I got stuck in this imaging, and over and over it repeated, my throat being slit and the blood pouring out. It was disgusting and terrifying imagery made up of a lot of fears all rolled into one.

When I left therapy, I realized that I was concerned about my mammogram tomorrow. I kept envisioning my breast being cut off with a knife. I kept hearing a nagging voice in the back of my head, "It's probably fine but what if it's not?"

Things are also starting to weigh a little bit heavier with thinking of going back to work next week. How will I keep my stress levels down between work and home responsibilities so that I can continue to heal properly? As I drove home, there was an old man walking along the side of the road with a cane. My imagery showed me running him over with the car, for no reason or purpose at all, just to scare myself that these intrusive thoughts were coming back to try to take over.

When you feel anxiousness and stress coming on, what do you do? Right now, I want to hide under my covers until I feel better. Unfortunately, that isn't an option. I guess the first step is to recognize that it is happening, as that is a piece that I missed a lot in the past. I tend to carry on without giving any attention to what might be bothering me. But I sometimes hesitate to do this, because it feels like the more you take notice of it, the more that it wants to control you. Even so, I know it's best to recognize what is happening before I start to slip down the side of the mountain and into the hole.

I have a lot more support than I used to. That has been something I've gained throughout these last few months by telling people close to me the struggles I have endured. I guess I just have to know what to do with that support and with my own recognition when things start to spiral.

I imagine myself right now peeking out the top of the hole and I see glimpses of the real world. I can see trees, birds, and some of the snow that has recently fallen on the ground. I imagine myself looking below me, back where I came from. There it was dark, black, and cold. The violent imaging and self-hatred were like thick black dust choking me down there. It was hard to breathe and hard to believe that I could make the climb. I don't ever want to see something that dark again. If you find yourself in this dark hole, know that even if it doesn't look like there is anything on the dirt walls to propel you up, there is. You might have to ask for help. That was probably my hardest thing to accept, that I had to yell until somebody heard me.

So please if this is you, please yell, don't whisper, don't cry, yell. Yell until the dirt walls echo, scream until the black dust gets out of your lungs. There is no way out alone. As the supplies and ropes start dropping in, know that you are safe, there is a way out and you now have so many other people helping you out of the hole. Let them help. Rest your weight if you need to and just let them carry you. It reminds me of the story of the man looking at his footprints in the sand. He asks God why there is only one set of footprints, as God had promised to walk beside him always. "When you saw one set of footprints, that was when I carried you," God told him. Sometimes you have to let your people carry you.

I thanked my friends the other night for being there in my darkest hours, and their response was, "You would do the same for us in a heartbeat." That is correct. When I am strong and you are weak, I will help carry you through. When I am weak again, I know that I can be carried, that there is a line up at the top of the hole with food, water, a stretcher, a blanket, an ambulance and everyone is there to hold me until I am well again. I know that though I lie down on the stretcher with all my bruises, I will be up walking in no time.

You are worth it. Do it for the little girl or little boy in you who wanted everything life had to offer. Scream for that child, scream and yell to give them a regular life that they deserve. They don't deserve the tragedy, torment and torture of this illness. They deserve a chance to see the sun as they once saw it when they were little, playing catch on a sunny day. Give that person their dreams back, fight for them. They did nothing to deserve this, and you can do everything to make it right.

As for me glimpsing the world from the top of the hole, I must remember that all I need to do is reach my arms out and all the tools I need are right there. I am surrounded by friends and family, and I am free to take a walk in the sunshine, do yoga, or have a nap. Not every day will be me running at full speed, and some days I'll be able to sit back and give myself some grace for things that are happening around me at the moment, breathe, feel my feet on the ground and carry on.

****

I had lots of apprehension about going for another mammogram. As it turns out, the appointment was terrible, but not because of my results. I sometimes feel stunned at the lack of empathy I experience in our current healthcare system. My doctor and the surgeon had wanted to get a second mammogram repeated three months after my last one. This has nothing to do with me, but is a decision made by two professionals in the medical industry. Yet like so many times before, when I arrive, I find that they have not received my paperwork, even though I double checked before the appointment that it had been sent. Then they become frustrated with me for some reason. Finally the paperwork is sorted out and I head in for the mammogram. But the technician just looks at me as if I were some entitled princess who is just using the health care system for fun and jollies.

Then comes the first question, the dreaded question: what are you doing here? When I explain what I am doing there, she begins to question everything. She tells me that she thinks it is ridiculous that the doctors are repeating this at three months, and that they should have waited a year, as was originally proposed after my first mammogram. I tell her that it is because they are being extra careful because I have some signs and because I am on add-back estrogen.

Then I get annoyed. Why am I the one explaining myself for my doctor's decisions like I am on trial? I feel judged, not worthy to be there, a waste of her time and even worse as she explains it to the radiologist and I overhear her saying that this doesn't need to be done right now. Now I worry that he will be biased when looking at my images, and will question why my doctors have a concern. I feel like he will think that he knows better than them, and by extension, me. Of course it will all be taken out on me because I am the one standing there with my shirt wide open and my boob hanging in a vice grip.

I know that my doctor has told me that in the past, he has seen reports that were clearly wrong. He ordered them to be re-done and when they were, it was found that the patient did in fact have cancer. Had he not trusted his gut, she would be dead right now. So I find it ironic that when I get my report back, which luckily shows that I have nothing more than benign calcifications, I also read a note that I have a "new bone" in my chest in the triangle chest muscle and through my armpit. I read it and think, "What? Excuse me? All of a sudden now I have grown a new bone in my chest?"

The funny thing is that it was completed by a radiologist and reviewed by another radiologist, and they both signed off on it. I was trying to figure out how I had grown a new bone when it hit me. The word "bone" was supposed to be "pain"! I remembered telling the tech when she asked why I was there about my new pain.

So, tell me, now do you think my doctor has a right to question mammogram reports that don't make sense?

My main point here is that in the last five years, most of the treatment I have received from my doctor and most places has been great, but then there are these gaslighting instances which are so frustrating and make you feel like scum. Why should the ones who are nice to you be a surprise, and the ones who rip you up be expected?

The next day at my internal specialist appointment for my swelling legs, I was expecting the same rhetoric, to be asked, "Why are you here?" by someone who never read my chart or any of my history. I expected to have to start from square one again, spill my guts to them, and then hear that there is nothing they can do for me and that I am in the wrong place. Or maybe they'll tell me my doctor is overreacting and I need to just live with this.

However, to my surprise, both the intern and the specialist had read my history of ischemic colitis and were prepared with some answers for me even before I arrived. Wow! I was blown away. I had not expected to be treated like a human being, and I had already prepared my answer to their question, "What brings you here today?" I was going to say, "I just wanted to visit my daughter in university so I was looking for an excuse to come for a long drive. I thought I'd just get the government to pay you $1,000 to look at me for five minutes and tell me you haven't read my history and I'm just in the wrong place and there is nothing wrong with me." Thankfully I didn't have to do that this time, as these two were as professional as the Mayo Clinic staff were when I went there.

    I don't know if this is mostly a women's issue, but it is so incredibly frustrating. It makes me sad for all of us being made to feel ashamed for clogging up their system. I say "their system" but darn it, it is our system, ours! We pay the tax money so that our health needs can be taken care of in a timely manner. They know that early detection saves lives, but they would rather wait until you have purple and green discharge coming out of your nipples to show they care.

    What do we do about it? I'm writing about my frustration, but really, what do I do about it? I think I am always afraid to tell them how I actually feel about how they are treating me because I am afraid they will treat me much worse. But I'm at the point now where I think, "Who cares?" I think the mammogram clinic has a bias against me anyway, so I swear if this happens again, I want to look them in the eyes and say, "This is my doctor's requisition and right now you are making me feel like I am unwanted here, and that I should be ashamed for coming in. Can you give him a call or write him a letter and tell him that you don't believe I belong here?" I wonder if that would do it? Or if it would make them even worse, so that they would also spit on the mammogram machine or squeeze just a little bit harder and a little bit longer? Regardless, I think this polite Canadian has to stop accepting being kicked around like a dog and stand up for myself, as well for my daughters and other women in the future. I will be the Karen against medical gaslighters as we all should, because we all deserve better!

TMS Session 38

I feel like my appetite is coming back and I want it to quit. I feel fatter already just thinking about it. My face feels rounder, my cheeks more full, my stomach is straining against my yoga pants. I probably gained weight in the last couple of days because I felt like eating…how stupid am I? I'll never fit those jeans as well as I did last year. Last week they were just starting to fit again and then I go and blow it!

The depression has eased up a lot in so many of my insecurities, but when it comes to weight and body image I still have so many insecurities. They run so deep that I don't know how long it could take to be comfortable in my own skin. I'm not pleased at all that my appetite has come back as it means I'm going to have to work much harder again at not gaining weight.

Do I have such a hard time with weight because I don't want to put the work into it? The thought that I'm lazy just pops into my head.

"Nope," I think, "No negative talk. You aren't lazy."

Okay, then why is it so hard? Now that my violent thoughts are getting better and my mind is clearer, I almost feel as if I have deliberately kept my weight as the one thing I could always hate about myself. If it's true that I am smart, I am kind, I am loving, I am fun, I am a great wife, mother, friend, worker, then I have to make sure that I have something I can hate myself for. But I wonder, if I stopped doing that, would I actually love myself? If I actually did weigh 140 pounds, would that be the very last thing, and then life would be absolutely perfect?

Of course it wouldn't be perfect. There are all kinds of uncertainties in life. Why would I assume that if I was the perfect weight, all would be well and I could finally offer myself unconditional love? From my very first journal I started writing when I was 12, I mention that I am overweight. It's like it's my identity.

So I ask myself this: can you love yourself and still be overweight? Your BMI says you're obese. You see cottage cheese in your arms and legs, and your belly where your C-section scar hangs over your underwear and feels like a big-ass bowl of pudding. There is an extra chunk of skin hanging from your neck and now of all things, you've started to get wrinkles around your eyes. Can you accept this person?

Maybe I could, but I'm afraid that if I accept that I look good enough, I'll let my guard down and just get fatter. This is a valid fear. Whenever I have lost weight in the past and gotten to a point where I feel like I look good enough, I start to feel good about myself. When that happens…wham! Within a few days I start packing on the pounds, and then more and more and more. I let myself eat what I want, I give myself treats. When I feel like I've done something good, I think I deserve some chips. Then that food tastes so good, I need another helping. I'm doing great, so it won't hurt.

I think weight is so perplexing because it is so complex and tied up with society's perspectives of people. I have read studies where people actually believe that people who are overweight are lazy, stupid, and worthless. I've read other surveys that found that people who are not overweight are treated better everywhere they go. So Uber drivers, flight attendants, bank tellers and shop associates are all nicer to people who are not overweight. Why is that? Race and weight are somehow similar in how they are false predictors of who you are. They are overgeneralizations that show the deep hidden biases that we all secretly share. How do we break down things that have been ingrained in us and passed down for generations?

I guess for one we could recognize that we have these biases. What if you had a lump on your big toe that you'd had since you were little, and your parents and everyone around you said that it was just a birthmark and nothing to worry about. As you get older, do you question it? Do you believe exactly what they said, even though you have heard that bumps like that could be cancerous? How deep does what others tell you have to do with your behavior? I know that if this happened to me, I'd wonder about the bump as I got older, and I'd wonder if my parents were indeed correct. I would take it upon myself to do my own research about it. I'd go to a professional to double check that my parents' theories were in fact correct. I would take accountability and look after myself. After all, my parents didn't have the same resources that we have now.

Do we do that with some of the biases that we had when we were children? Don't you think it's up to us as adults to research the truth and acknowledge what are biases actually are? I'm not saying we have to blame our parents, but I don't think that just because we are raised a certain way it means that we can never change.

Where do you think we got the overweight bias from? In statues from hundreds of years ago, women with large stomachs, legs, and arms were celebrated as goddesses. Somehow over the years it became a sign of being fat and lazy. Even from a young age, I can see in my journal that I was told I had a big butt and that my hips were as wide as the TV. I remember looking at pictures of myself and knowing that I was putting on weight. I knew that if you put on weight it meant people would look at you like you weren't as good as them.

Cheers to those who can eat small quantities or have fabulous metabolisms, those who go to the gym every day, walk, jog and make quinoa with salmon and asparagus for dinner each night. The rest of us losers are too lazy to go to the gym every day, we are too lazy to make fresh home cooked vegetables and count the ounces of protein in our meals, we are gluttonous, we are pigs, we stuff our faces until we cannot breathe. We shovel in 76 chips by the time others have put on their running shoes, we scarf down 45 chocolates by the time others have cleaned the asparagus. We are disgusting humans.

What is sad is that I actually believe that about myself, and that is precisely the problem.

I think about the mountain analogy again, except the lake hidden on the other side is the perfect body. What if making all the changes you need to is too overwhelming…it would feel like hiking with a backpack of 100 extra pounds. What if instead of taking that backpack I chose a smaller one, with just a few things in it? Would I then be able to make it up the mountain? Would I turn around in defeat at the first incline if I carried less? What if I just picked one thing to take up the mountain for now? What if the only things in my backpack were doing yoga and walking a few times a week? I would be so proud when I made it to the top of the mountain! Looking back down the trail, I would know I never would have made it with all the extra things in the backpack. So the next time I hike the mountain, I'll put drinking eight glasses of water in my backpack. I can handle that.

Now after two hikes I have made two big changes. On the next hike I start with eating more vegetables. That's it, nothing else, just eat more vegetables. Not a full diet that would make the backpack too heavy but just a simple eat more vegetables. Now I have done the hike three times, and I am getting stronger. I know that if I had started with all of the expectations in the backpack, I would never have made it. I would have slid back down the mountain, my legs aching, sweat pouring from my brow. I would have sworn never to go up that mountain again. The difference this time is that I changed one thing about how I approached the journey – I took on fewer responsibilities. That is the only way I was able to be successful.

So, if I do this, will I love myself in the end? I don't know, but I certainly will be much kinder to myself. Instead of berating or bullying myself, saying I'm not good enough, I get healthier at my own pace. Which brings me back to the bias. Imagine another person who starts the hike has 100 pounds in their backpack. They are carrying guilt, shame, substance abuse, bad parents, and grief, and it is weighing them down. When they start climbing up the mountain, they fall down, and then they give up. Do we laugh at them and call them losers? Do we stare at them and think, "Get your disgusting shit together"? Why can't we be kind, knowing that their journey has been different from ours?

What about the girl who goes to the gym five times a week and looks fit and healthy, but who in reality throws up after she eats and hates living in her own skin? When she is in public, people only see the outside. How can our outsides determine who is winning or losing life? We should be kind to the thin girl who hates herself and is bulimic and we should be kind to the overweight girl who fights depression and violent image OCD, and tries as hard as she can to make it through one more day.

I think about what I would tell myself if I was an outsider or friend:

Maybe one day she can start thinking about what to take in the backpack, but for now she has a lot of other stuff going on and I should give her the grace to carry on getting well. For now, if she walks the trail at the bottom of the mountain, crosses the bridge with the beautiful stream and has gratitude for being at the bottom of the mountain, that's enough for her. I don't expect her to climb the mountain when she has been in the dark for so long and she has fought so hard to just see the grass. The mountain can wait. I'm going to look at her differently. I'm going to celebrate that she is still here, laughing and playing games with her kids. She is seeing positives instead of negatives and she has so much to live for. I don't want to push her right now. I'm going to be kind to her and let her know that she did a great job just getting through the last seven weeks of TMS therapy and all the other challenges. The non-dimpled thighs can wait. They may never be non-dimpled, and even if they aren't I want her to know she is no loser at life. She blew the lid off her depression and OCD and now I just want her to enjoy how far she has come. I have a feeling that making a pathway for the depression may make a pathway for body image as well, and I am done kicking her when she is down.

****

As I have broken open my story of my life with OCD and depression, I find myself looking at a new person in the mirror. While I am the same little smiley girl, the same energetic student, worker, and mother that I always was, I am different. I have let a large inner circle in on secrets that I have held for 28 years. It kind of feels like that nightmare that lots of people have, where you are standing in front of a room full of people and you're naked. All your private parts, dimples, and wrinkles are exposed for the world to see. You try to hide or cover yourself and it's terrifying.

When strangers are looking at you though, who do they see? A middle aged woman's body with all its imperfections and scars and I would say most of them aren't judging what they see on the outside but are as mortified for you as you are for you. As you stand there red in embarrassment and try to back up and hide behind whatever podium, desk or backing you can find, they too are closing their eyes for you, and they feel so terrible and so empathetic to you standing there naked. You can see even the horror on their faces, it matches your own. Some are not looking because they just can't, they are so horrified that they are hiding their own faces. Some are looking to help you, they run in different directions to try to find your clothes or something for you to hide behind. Some just feel so sad for you that they want to cry for you. Some have a nervous laughter like they can't believe this is happening and it's funny but shocking and sad at the same time, they don't know whether to clap or walk out. Which totally reminds me of the Oscars and the slap heard around the world. When people are faced with a reaction they look to each other for help, should we laugh, should we be angry, should we be upset, or should we do nothing at all? We are all social creatures, and, in a group, we don't want to be the outlier, the one that was yelling for security while the other thousand people were giving a standing ovation.

    I feel like for some members of my inner circle, seeing my authentic self makes them want to look away and pretend they don't see me standing naked. They are so mortified for me that they want to pretend they don't know that naked person. They want the naked person to just put their clothes back on and pretend like this never happened. They feel like if they do that, everyone can just go on with their lives like before. They are the ones I find it hardest to come to terms with, because it feels like me being honest is shameful and embarrassing for them.

    There are the ones who laugh nervously and have no idea how to react. They look to the rest of the crowd to try to figure out what to do. I can empathize with and understand this group. I also freeze up in surreal moments and don't know how to react. It takes some time to assess the situation and come up with a response, but it feels more accepting and kind that they really just don't know what to say. After all, we are all human and we don't always say or do the right things. These people just need a little more time.

    Then there are the ones who stand up out of the crowd and start running to help find your clothes and help find somewhere to hide you. Those are the real heroes. They don't think about the rest of the crowd, they just want to do anything to protect you. Whether they know you or not, they empathize with the situation you are in and immediately want to help. They offer words of encouragement and support, tell you not to worry, then they find your clothes and help you put them on.

Who would you be in the crowd? Who would you want to be? When it was me standing up there naked and embarrassed, I was ashamed. I wanted to say to that girl, "What the hell are you doing? Why are you embarrassing yourself and others by telling your secrets and exposing your privates to the world?"

Then I looked again at that girl, and I realized that I knew why she was doing it. It's because she realizes that there are two options: bare your soul and tell people about your struggle, or bury yourself deeper in pretending that nothing is wrong. When you admit what is going on, you're naked and exposed. But the other way is to pile on more clothes. The people who do that are covered in layers, the sun beats down and makes them hot. They feel like they can't take another minute. Sweat is pouring from their faces. They are so exhausted sometimes it hurts for them to breathe from the weight of the clothes and the heat. They know that they can't keep living that way but they are too ashamed to take their clothes off.

Those are the people I want to take my clothes off for. I want to show them that I was able to shed that burden and keep on living. But I also wanted to do it for myself. I couldn't carry the weight of the layers anymore. I wanted to be free so I could breathe. I could say I was drunk when I took off my clothes. I could say that I was in such a horrible place that I had no choice but to strip naked. Or I could look at it as an opportunity for myself and for others who have too many layers on.

So who do I want to be? I want to be the one in the crowd who jumps up and tries to help the next person who doesn't even know that they have the power to take off their layers and breathe. After they undress, I want to be there to help them find lighter clothes, possibly just a large umbrella. I want them to know that I accept them just the way they are, as well as the better version of themselves that they are going to be.

It doesn't matter about the people that are ashamed of them and are hiding. As it turns out, those people are wearing a lot more layers than they need to. They also feel uncomfortable with all their layers, but ignore it because they could never, ever, ever stand in front of someone naked. No matter how hot and sweaty they become, they would rather sweat to death than be known for standing up naked. If only they could see that standing there naked comes with so many benefits. For one thing, it's really cool and breezy! You also find so much support from the people running to help you. Those are the people who soar with you, shedding happy tears that you have done it. You have braved what you never imagined you could do.

TMS Session 39

This week I am back at work, as my full time treatments are over. I feel generally pretty good, but just like coming back to work after vacation, the habit must sink in again. I've had a really quiet life over the past eight weeks. I was able to slow my pace completely down, just doing treatments, writing, getting exercise, and cleaning and cooking at no great pace for my family. I felt no rush and no panic. I felt little stress. I loved the feeling of peace that I got from that experience. Going back to my work routine, with meetings and things coming at me from both work and home, was without a doubt overwhelming.

To add to the stress of it all, on the Monday after I finished a day of working from home and was resting my brain on the couch, Kevin let me know that we were sorting calves that night. We needed to sort the older ones from the younger ones and determine which ones were to go on the truck to be sold tomorrow. He wanted me to get dinner ready so we could eat and then get back outside by 5:45 to get started before it got too dark. My first job was to back up the truck to the fifth wheel cattle trailer. I am terrible at backing up anything, but I thought if I just kept practicing, I would get it. It turned out that there was a patch of ice, and every time I would get close to the ball to hitch, the truck would slide a foot away from it. Kevin came out and tried, and he couldn't get it either. This kind of work can be really frustrating, as it feels like we are always running against some kind of clock. Besides the usual time worries families face – getting to an appointment on time, picking someone up from school – farm families have even more. We're always fighting the clock in all different ways, getting things finished before the last day of warm weather, or like tonight, before night falls. It is a stressful way of life when you feel you can't take your time to get a job done right.

We ended up leaving the truck and headed to the barnyard to start sorting, There were a bunch of calves already in the barnyard, but Brant decided he needed to show me how he could jump off the fence into a pile of snow. His loud *Watch me, Mom!* and my loud *Be quiet Brant! You'll scare the cows!* was enough to start a stampede, and all the calves left the barnyard. Even though I knew this was going to cause us to have to go even later, with everything I've learned over the past few months, I decided to try a different approach to my usual getting stressed. I told Kevin, "We need to breathe. Tell Brant we are sorry but an eight year old doesn't need to be in the middle of this. Mom and Dad are stressed trying to beat the clock and need to focus on getting this done."

The mood changed from there. We even shared a laugh later when I was busily trying to open a rolling gate and I didn't get away from the tire in time and it tripped me. I fell smack into the snow and manure, and Kevin told me with a laugh, "There's no lying down on the job!" I laughed too, and so did Brant. The rest of the time it went as smoothly as it does every time you sort. (That's sarcasm.) It started getting dark and we were almost done, but sorting this black steer one from that black heifer was getting harder and harder. We finished though, but between going back to my job that day and doing that all evening, I was completely spent.

The next day I went into the office to work and I had a lot of apprehension. The last day I had been in the office I'd ended up going to emergency as I felt my suicidal thoughts were becoming real and I was making a plan to make it happen. I tried to push through, because I felt like I had to make it past that hump. My co-workers had pasted pictures of themselves in funny little places all over my office, which really helped take my mind off of it being my first office day back. I had a big meeting coming up at 10:00 a.m. and my mind had started to churn trying to get ready for it. Then my stomach decided it was going to join the party because why let the brain have all the cortisol fun? So, I ended up on a run to the bathroom right before the meeting and I didn't think it was going to let up as I sat in the bathroom stall. I decided to call it out for what it was – nerves!

Even so, my first inclination was to think, "I have to get home so I can be near a toilet. How could I think I was ready for going back to work?" But I knew I had positive thoughts in there, so I pulled them up and said, "No, stomach. I got this and you are going to stop now. I'm going to take deep breaths on my walk back to the office and you will settle and I will continue on with my meeting." Guess what? It worked! My stomach started to settle, and I began getting immersed in work questions. However, it didn't last long. By noon, I was a mess. I went to my friend Shelly's for lunch and did the yoga cat pose on her linoleum kitchen floor while she made some hot soup. I felt so spent, but after the hot bowl of soup and her loving smile, I felt much better. She sat and listened with a funny grin while I talked about some things that she would have loved to comment more fully on but instead shook her head and just offered silence and support. It was enough for me to make it to the afternoon. I struggled again after lunch, but by 3:00 p.m., I had asked another friend out for coffee, and as we walked and the crisp, cold air hit my face, I felt I could make it to the end of the day.

When Ava picked me up from work, I was frazzled, like I was so overstimulated that I couldn't even possibly remember if we needed milk from the grocery store and in that moment, I honestly didn't care. When I got home at 5:00 p.m., I crawled into my bed and covered my head. As a joke I told the family I'd see them tomorrow. I knew what I needed though – peace and utter quiet. I needed to be kind to myself and not feel guilty for not making supper or cleaning. Tonight I just needed to look after myself enough so that I could go back tomorrow. It worked! I got up later and did a Yin yoga video to regulate my nervous system and the calm and peace started to come back.

From there, the rest of the week just got better. I proved to myself that I could stick it out and take what I learned and apply it in the moments that I needed it. It was such a great achievement to be able to do that for myself. I'm sure it sounds mediocre in some people's minds, but for me, this was taking control of a beast of habitual pattern, and it felt so empowering!

On Friday night we were headed to a potluck supper and cattle meeting with our cattle group. This group has met since the girls were little, and while some of the faces have changed, it has been pretty much a constant for many years. It is a time to share stories and things you have learned on the farm and lean on each other's expertise and experience. Kevin had asked me if I was going to share with the group all that I have gone through with my mental health. I wasn't totally sure that I could, but ultimately since it is my dream and passion to be a mental health advocate, I decided to go ahead. So in front of 15 onlookers I came forward with my authentic self and told what I have been through during TMS treatments. After I told them that I wanted to end the stigma and that I was feeling much better, they all clapped. I felt exhausted with giving that of myself but I also felt victorious in knowing that I absolutely want to help others. I hope that I can reach people at a younger age so they can get the help they deserve much earlier than I did. I can't buy back my thousands of hours of violent imaging distressing and disrupting my life, but maybe I can do that for someone else. Maybe just by hearing about my journey they can begin to be free.

While it's true that I am afraid of being looked at differently I am not ashamed. I wasn't given this terrible disease so I could hide in the corner and let it beat me. Sometimes I start to experience self-doubt about putting this all out there because I am more afraid now of what others will think of my family and my kids. I don't want this to affect them negatively. But I feel a pull that is so strong. It tells me that I was meant for this, and that all the time I suffered was not for nothing.

I don't want to be angry and humiliated about these mental health diseases. My ancestors who suffered like I do had to be ashamed; they had no chance to be accepting of their illnesses because back then no one accepted anyone different. Hitler wanted disabled people, gay people and anyone who was different to be put to death along with the Jews. It continued in Canada and throughout the world, maybe not as extreme as being put to death, but being locked away in institutions or being humiliated and shamed to be a "normal" person. There were likely people in history who had they told anyone what their thoughts were like, would have been stoned or burned to death. The world we live in now is much more of a "stand up to hate" world than it has ever been before. While it's not true everywhere, you have to start somewhere.

I am not the first to come forward, but I want to be in the line of those who speak out and tell their truth. I want my children, my nieces and nephews, and all children to know that we are so much more than our brains and physical parts. We have so much technology, support and help that others never had. We can live full, happy, productive lives and still have a mental illness. I got a life sentence with Harm OCD and depression – it may come and go but it will never be truly cured.

I know my path is difficult and there will be darkness again, but there will also be celebrations. And besides, I have so much support now for the dark times, and I don't want anyone to feel alone in their darkness. I want them to look up at the sky from Australia, Nigeria, Chile, Hong Kong, Romania, and I want them to see the same stars that I am looking at and know that none of us are alone in our illnesses. I always thought I was so unique until I started uncovering other peoples' stories. It was sadly validating to know that the disgusting and grotesque things that were in my mind had been seen by others in extremely similar ways. You may know someone else has had cancer, but I never knew for the last 28 years that someone else had cyclical disturbing thoughts of harming themselves and others.

I'm hoping my book reaches all those people in the world who think that they are alone. I want them to know that that they can stop hating themselves, because what they have is a treatable illness. Even if they don't have access to treatments, reading my book could be therapy enough to fight against the darkness in their brain and know that they have the power to overcome it. The first step is to know you have it, the second is to face it squarely. Then once you get to the sources of your fears, you have the ability to overcome them and stop their power. The time is now.

****

I always felt like I was so different, with my horrific imaging cycling around my thoughts and horrifying me through many periods of my life. I knew it wasn't normal, but I thought it was somehow part of life, and that the things that started in university were just a one off that I would never have to think about again. I pushed the horror of it all back in deep so I wasn't constantly questioning myself and could go ahead and live life. I knew it was there, but I didn't want to admit it to myself. Admitting it to myself meant that I had to do something about it and ultimately, I had to tell people about it. I had such high expectations of myself that I never wanted to admit the truth of who I was inside. I think I was honestly more afraid of my own judgement than anyone else's. Admitting it was such a difficult step. But my only regret is that I didn't do it sooner.

However, I do feel like some things are meant to be. As awful as it sounds, I was meant to hold onto this for 28 years, because I was going to do something with it afterwards. If I had never struggled this hard, I never would have known what others with this illness have gone through or why their life had to end by suicide. Now I can wholly and completely understand it.

After all these years I am so used to my Harm OCD thoughts that I don't even recognize some of them as being part of it. I knew that seeing people or myself being stabbed, hung or drowned was definitely not right. But just yesterday I realized that I still have some thoughts that I don't even realize are unusual. I was driving down our grid road to get to another town to pick up Chinese food. At the end of our lane, I looked left, and I looked right, and in my thoughts, I saw a car smash into us because I thought I hadn't looked closely enough. After driving another eight kilometers, I went to turn left at a yield sign on a busy grid, and again I looked left and right. Then as I turned, I saw in my mind a grain truck smash into us. I kept driving and I got to a stop sign at the highway, and I looked left and right, then I looked left and right again, then I looked a third time to be sure the sun wasn't in my eyes or something was blocking me from seeing. As I crossed the highway I could physically feel the crunch of the oncoming car slamming into my vehicle as the car went into a spin. The side was smashed in and the glass shattered. I looked back at Brant with glass and blood on his face to see if he was okay. This all happened in my head in the split second it took me to cross the highway. It happens to me all the time but I am so accustomed to it that I never even react to it. I don't wonder why. I don't think, "Stop it!" I don't think anything, I just keep driving. I'm hungry, and I can't wait to get that Chinese food.

I am sad that I never even thought of putting this in my script for TMS. I am sad that I didn't even know that it wasn't normal to imagine this hundreds of times while driving. I have been smashed into with a semi probably a million times. It has never stopped, and the funniest thing is that this is the very first time in all these years that I realized I never even give it a second thought. I just live with it. What if I could drive peacefully? What if I never had to imagine being hit at every single intersection and with every semi coming toward me. Wow, that must feel wonderful.

    Maybe I am so hypervigilant because I have a fear of being in a car accident. But where is the line between hypervigilance and just normal, careful driving? No wonder I'm always so exhausted after long trips! There have been times I can barely function when I get somewhere because my thoughts have overwhelmed the crap out of me. Imagine the cortisol I must produce from the stress of constantly being in a car accident! I'm just blown away that all this time I didn't even know how awful it was for me. It seems like I am always uncovering pieces of my disease that I can work on. I'm worried now because here at my 39th TMS treatment this is just coming to my attention. What else is there that could be changed to help me live better?

    I guess my journey isn't really over, and likely never will be. I will fix one piece at a time, and maybe that is all I can handle anyway. If the entire car is broken and you try to fix everything at one time, you won't be able to do it. If my brain has been broken for this long, I need to give it one new part at a time. First the transmission, then the motor, then the brakes, and eventually I'll get to the radio. The most important thing is to get it running first, and then I will fix the little details as they come up. Little by little I will be drivable again.

TMS Session 40

I've struggled this week. I've been sad, very anxious, and have had to try hard to control my Harm OCD thoughts. I have for the most part kept them away, but they snuck in a lot this week. I think self-doubt has creeped in, and along with it the thoughts come and try to get some self-torture going.

I had terrible nightmares on Monday night. They were relentless. In the first one, I was being shot at it in a vehicle while trying to hide in the floorboards, and the glass was smashing with the bullets coming through the car. Like in all the classic nightmares I have, I'm running and hiding, watching others get shot and die in front of me before I am the last to get shot, and then I wake up just before it happens. I wake with a fright and I can't get back to sleep as the torturous images go through my mind and make my heart race.

A few hours later I fall into my next dream, where I don't have any eyebrows and I can't figure out why. I keep trying to draw eyebrows on, but everyone is looking and laughing at the way I have drawn them.

I wake up from that and then in the next one I get into a car with my dad and brother Ron. We are driving on a beach road and the waves start coming over the car, pulling us deeper into the ocean. As the car fills up with water, I hold my breath and try to keep swimming. Then when I feel I can swim no longer and have no breath left, I wake up.

That whole night had me waking up experiencing that heavy weight behind my eyes and feeling like I had been punched in the stomach and head. All I wanted was a do-over where I would get some sleep. However, I had work to do, and I had to get in the shower and get rolling. After all I've been through and with going back to work and trying to get back on top of things, I don't even imagine it as an option to not push myself to get to work.

When I arrived, I felt so tired and my eyes were so heavy I just wanted to close them. If only I could transport myself back under my covers and console myself that everything would be alright. I just needed some rest. There was a meeting with one of my staff scheduled for 11:00, but I called and asked her if we could do it earlier because I just needed to see her smiley face on Teams. I also needed to get into a conversation about our work projects because that would help me to keep pressing on. It worked! I also did some deep breathing and positive thinking. "It's okay, Michelle, a few more hours and you can cover your head, cuddle up into a fetal position, fall asleep and hope for a reset."

Falling asleep is my reset. I don't know what I would do without it. Sleep brings me comfort, and that is the self-care that I want. The peace to just not be me, even for just a half-hour nap, allows me to get up and be me again, until I get to go back to being unconscious again.

You might be wondering if I have so many nightmares why do I like to sleep? Wouldn't I be scared to sleep? The funny thing is that I see it as sleep-Michelle's problem, not mine. She takes over while my awake narrator gets a break. The problem is that sleep-Michelle and awake-Michelle share the same brain, so in reality, the stress and problems that awake-Michelle has don't disappear, they just get re-lived, re-hashed, mutated, garbled, and processed somewhere way back in the storage compartments of my brain. I just hope that the pathways I build with TMS therapy apply to the sleep brain as well, and hopefully the logical part of my brain will catch on to the nightmares and say, "What the torturous hell is going on over there?? It's not right. Leave her alone."

I believe when I am stressed and don't even realize it, the first place it comes out is in my nightmares. I think completing day 40 of my TMS treatment has me doubting how healed I am. All the doubts keep popping in – *you're not well, you have a mental illness, you're not better, you can't work, you can't function, you can't…you can't…you can't…* I still worry, even though the treatment has gone well and my psychiatrist's assessment shows me passing OCD and depression with flying colors! So why doesn't it feel like that this week?

****

I decided to Google *depression symptoms* again and found that symptoms of depression include angry outbursts, irritability or frustration, even over small matters. For the most part over the TMS treatment I have felt pretty good in this regard. However, in the last couple of weeks with being back to work, working with the cows, doing taxes, looking after the house and trying to do my self-care, I've had a sinking feeling. I'm trying to do everything I've been told to do – take time for me, do yoga, write, have some alone time – but I still have this anxious edge, and I feel ready to snap at anyone who does something that upsets me. Well today I snapped at lunch, and it was just as the symptoms described above, over a very small matter.

Just like any other marriage, Kevin and I have pet peeves about each other. One thing that sets me off is when someone tampers with food that to me is perfect just the way it is. Kevin used to find the chocolate milk in the jug too chocolatey for him, so he would pour some regular milk into the chocolate milk jug. I would walk to the fridge expecting my perfectly cold, perfectly chocolatey chocolate milk and I'd be met with a light tan jug of regular white milk with a hint of chocolate that I couldn't even taste! It drove me madder than a cat trying to catch her tail. After many outbursts from me over the last 30 years he no longer does this. However, he still pours white cold milk all over the prepared Kraft Dinner on his plate, so he is eating a light cheesy version of pig slop. I ignore it because he does it in his own plate. As long as mine is still perfectly cheesy, as God and the makers of the Kraft Dinner recipe intended, then I leave him alone. My motto is if you want to do something your way, go ahead, just don't wreck mine.

Well, my mom had made us my favorite beef barley soup with the perfect amount of brown gravy flavoring, and I loved it! As I went to microwave some soup for lunch, I saw that someone had been messing around with some leftover white Cracker Barrel Cheese Kraft Dinner. First of all, who would mess with that recipe? Second of all, someone also poured white milk into the container of Kraft Dinner, and it had pooled all along the bottom of the container. It made my stomach turn just walking by it, but I continued on, excited about having my good perfect tasty soup. As I walked to the microwave, I noticed Kevin was putting this heathen Kraft Dinner macaroni into his soup! Well, I think he is an idiot but again, no harm, no foul to me. Until he takes his bowl, which he had already littered full of milky white cheese noodles, and mixed it into the soup! But the worst came next: he decided there was too much food in his bowl so he dropped a ladle full back into my mom's pot of perfect soup.

I lost it! It felt like anything I ever learned about being a good person was lost in that few minutes. I turned into a subhuman who acted like Snow White's poison apple had just been stewed into my soup.

"How dare you!!!" I yelled. I grabbed a spoon to quickly try to fish out all of the white creamy noodle contents that had wrecked my mother's perfect soup.

Ava and Dad chimed in. "Calm down! It's just noodles!"

I yelled, "It's not just noodles! It is milk-filled disgusting noodles affecting the taste of my soup!" I picked out every last piece of poison in the soup, then resumed my lunch, taking my soup and sitting down at the table.

As I tried to eat, I heard things like, "Mom, you are a psycho," "Mom, did you take your meds today?" "Mom, I thought you were going to smash all the bowls in the kitchen!" "Mom, what's the big deal?" Then Brant re-enacted my yell repeatedly as Kevin and Ava laughed. I said, "I think I should go and just live in a residential facility." They said, "They wouldn't even want you there; you are too crazy." I said, "Fine, I will go to my room, take a nap and try to become a better person in there."

The anxiousness, the nightmares, and the anger outbursts are all signs for me that I am leaving peaceful TMS therapy Michelle, Zen and grateful Michelle, in the dust as fast as the road runner. It has literally only been a few days since my last treatment, and I already have started to slide. What the hell is wrong with me and how do I get back to the Zen? I feel like the angry red-faced emoji with his top blown off. Why?

This particular obsession with food being left alone may be an OCD thing. The problem is not that I like my food the way I like it, the problem is that my reaction was intense for absolutely no reason. I could have walked over to Mom's container of soup and said politely, "I don't like that in my soup, Kevin. I'm just going to scoop it out," or I could have just said nothing at all and just eaten it. I could have avoided the soup for the rest of lunch and the family wouldn't have seen "the crazy" this afternoon.

We all have emotional outbursts. I've seen them from Kevin, Ava and Brant, and none of them are perfect saints. However I feel like I should be a role model for my kids. I know better than an eight year old and I should have more control then a hormonal teenager. Kevin, too, has his moments working outside where he turns into a frustrated werewolf. How do we bring this down a notch to be more Zen for the children who emulate us, as well as for our own mental health and well-being?

I guess first, we notice it, second, we know it is an issue, and third, if we admit the first two then we can take steps to do better next time. Just because I almost finished all this TMS treatment doesn't mean I get a card that says I am now perfectly emotionally adjusted.

But I might get a card that says:

Good for you. You finished this treatment. It is now up to you to work on controlling your thoughts and emotions. You may have good days and bad days. On the good days, enjoy your life, and on the bad days, try to turn them into good days before you write off the whole day. Try to nurture yourself with good food (lol), lots of hydration, calming activities, and maybe just give yourself a break. You have run the marathon and yet you can't sit still to say that you did it, instead you move on to all the other things you need to accomplish. If you run a marathon and then sit on your ass for the next six months, you can be sure your body will not be ready to run another marathon again. If you run the marathon though and then every day try to do a little bit to keep in shape, in six months, it won't take long at all to be ready to do that marathon again.

I'm going to try to enjoy the feeling of finishing the marathon without thinking ahead about which marathon I will do next. What if I sat back a bit and said, "Rest, my darling. You have accomplished great things. Resting is part of your healing. You want to forget how much pain and torture you endured. You want to mask and hide it. You want to say you are free, but you can't stay free unless you keep up with the lessons you learned. Stop being so darn hard on yourself. You can do this but first you need to remember that the tortoise won the race. The rabbit didn't win. He was cocky, self-centered, and felt invincible but the tortoise believed in himself. Even though it would take him longer, he could still win the race if he believed in himself. The tortoise didn't have negative voices in his head telling him there was no way he could do it. Now that I have learned how to quiet my voices, I can be happy and healthy, well-adjusted and stop my emotional outbursts. I just have to think like a tortoise."

TMS Complete

Recently I have experienced some very blissful moments, moments of outright joy. I'm excited for the future and all the possibilities it can bring. But sometimes it is still difficult for me to not want to party with my university teenager children and friends. I feel like if I'm not drinking with them, I have nothing fun to say and they won't want me around. Maybe I am just craving a past that is long gone, and I just have to adjust to my new reality. It's hard sometimes to accept that I am an almost 50-year-old mom. I'm not nineteen like they are. I think I want to feel that way again, but I just have to do it in different ways. I know I can when I'm dancing around the kitchen listening to music that I shouldn't be listening to like *Crazy Bitch* by Buckcherry. The wildness comes out of me with every taboo lyric like I am some big rebel. *Ooooh you are an old lady singing a swear, how wild of you!* However, in the moment that I am belting it out, I feel that same sense of freedom, the rebellious freedom of being a teenager.

   The truth is that I'm a long, long way from being a teenager. I always had a boyfriend, then a husband and then children, so I never really did have much of that wild freedom. Maybe that's why I sometimes crave it, like something I missed. My babies will never be babies again, I will never feel the kicks in my stomach, I will never hold my own newborn in my arms again, all the glorious and awful moments of being a mom with toddlers is over. I think you can grieve for the days gone by and the things that you will never do again, but at some point you have to pass it by and look forward to new experiences and new challenges. I look forward to seeing my daughters walk down the aisle, seeing their excitement of a new baby of their own on the way, holding a grandchild baby in my arms, hearing them say, "I love you, Grandma," those are all things that will be so precious and will come with some much love and excitement. Who is Brant going to be? Who will he take to his grad? Who will be his first girlfriend? What will he choose as a career? Will Kevin and I be able to have more freedom as we age and have time again for snowmobiling and more travelling?

   I think in order to enjoy the present, we cannot dwell on the days gone by nor be worried about the future. We need to relish in gratitude of the present, while feeling the blessings of the days gone by and blessings for what is to come.

It feels odd after 28 years of not knowing what was wrong with you and trying to deny and hide it to see TikTokers openly discussing their Harm OCD episodes. Their experiences are chillingly close to mine and it's hard to really comprehend that this isn't just me. To think that out of the billions of people on earth that I thought I was the only one terrorized by my cyclical violent imaging and now because of people speaking out, I know I am not alone. I am sad for the people who go through it like I did, but so grateful for them that they know what they have, and they aren't afraid to find others who have the same. It's opened up this whole new world to me that I didn't know ever existed. It's very validating to know that this truly is a disease and not somehow just something that I am making up in my mind.

The stigma is changing but not for all. A TikToker explained that she gets loving and supportive comments as well as very negative comments about how she is weak minded and should just use positive thinking to find a way out of this. Why are illnesses of the brain so misunderstood, when it is in fact a part of the human body that works or doesn't work depending on numerous factors?

Last night I was able to go to a family supper and for the whole entire day I had no violent imaging, not even one episode. When I don't notice it and I truly get to enjoy being in the moment it is such a relief, like when you take your ski boots off your feet after a day of skiing and you walk around so light and free. The worst times for me are quiet times, when I lay my head down at night or try to be absolutely still in yoga or meditation. It's getting a lot better, but the violent imaging is never gone and maybe it never will be. I just continually say *no* to it and eventually it seems to leave me for a while. The fact is, however, that my ability to say *no* to it and for it to leave me alone means that my pathways have been opened up thanks to TMS therapy and my high doses of medication. I am not stronger minded right now because of this, I am in remission from my disease. When my disease attacks again, I won't be able to say no any longer. Will I be weak then?

I don't think people who make negative comments about mental health conditions have any idea what it's like to live in the shoes of someone who does. So how could they possibly comprehend? I don't know what it is like to be blind, I don't know what it is like to have breast cancer, I don't know what it is like to have a colostomy bag, but I do know that whatever that condition is, you should be kind. How and why do people on social media feel that it is okay to harass and call you down for what you are? Whether it's race, weight, sexual orientation, or a medical condition, why would you be unkind to anyone, anywhere?

As a society it seems like we are always judging when we should be loving. Just because you think something, why do you have to say it? What do you gain from hurting someone else? Do you love yourself more because you are your own idea of perfection? I honestly don't understand it. But I do know that as I move forward wanting to help others, I am putting myself out there, and I will probably fall victim to the harsh critics. Which makes you wonder, why would you even put yourself in that position? The only reason is that you know it is the right thing to do. People who judge and criticize have never been in your shoes and will never understand what it is like to be you. Your job is not to help make them understand, you never will. Your one and only job is to help others who need help and to be proud of yourself that you did.

Conclusion so far

I've come a long, long way from a very dark breakdown. I don't think I am fully healed but I think I am getting better. Actually, "healed" isn't the correct word. I am the broken crayon. I can put tape around the crayon to fix it but ultimately it is still broken and one day the tape will no longer hold. For now though, I'm going to keep coloring, and I'm going to make some amazing pictures in the meantime.

We aren't who we were before the storms, we aren't who we are going to be in the future, but we are here trying every day. I want us to keep sharing our stories with each other and encouraging each other that the pictures we make are beautiful and meaningful no matter what they look like.

I'll meet you again soon to catch up,

Love,
Michelle

www.ingramcontent.com/pod-product-compliance
Lightning Source LLC
Chambersburg PA
CBHW050224100526
44585CB00017BA/1991